There is first the literature of knowledge, and secondly, the literature of power. The function of the first is to teach. The function of the second is — to move; the first is a rudder, the second an oar or a sail.

—deQuincy: *Essays on the Poets: Pope*

The Judgment Seat of Christ

Including General William Booth's Vision of Heaven

Rick C. Howard

Naioth Sound and Publishing
Woodside, California

Unless otherwise indicated, all scripture quotations are taken from *The New King James Version* of the Bible.

The Judgment Seat of Christ
ISBN 0-9628091-0-1
Copyright © 1990 by Rick C. Howard
Naioth Sound and Publishing
2995 Woodside Road, Suite 400
Woodside, CA 94062
U.S.A.

Published by Naioth Sound and Publishing
2995 Woodside Road, Suite 400
Woodside, CA 94062
U.S.A.

Dedication

To the Southern Baptist layman whose life and testimony gave a context for his warning — a warning
which changed my life!

✳

Contents

Author's Preface

It was a humid spring evening in Memphis, Tennessee. I had fallen asleep in my small studio apartment, still dressed in my street clothes, too exhausted emotionally and physically to change for bed.

Suddenly I was completely awake, my heart pounding fiercely and my clothes plastered to my body by perspiration! My eyes were wide open — as in a moment of terror — and I was crying!

I had just seen a vision of Jesus Christ for which I'd had no preparation. There was no "octave" or precedent in my life or study to truly understand what I had seen. Furthermore, the circumstances of the vision had struck me with fear: I was left shaken and afraid.

I knew where I had been! I knew what I had seen, and it was not the result of weariness or hunger. The place was Christ's *bema*, or Judgment Seat!

For reasons I will explain later, I had just spent four days studying every scripture and teaching I could find on that subject, and I knew the description of the place well. But I was completely unprepared for the drama and the terror of that moment.

The Christ I saw had flaming eyes of fire, and hair as refined, fuller-white wool. He bore no resemblance to the "gentle Jesus, meek and mild" whose picture had hung in my childhood bedroom.

But even more awesome and startling than His appearance was His *presence*. It evoked fear! *This was a place of terror!*

I lay awake, my mind racing down many corridors of

memory, afraid to move or lose the thought. This experience produced questions which demanded answers: Was such a picture of the Christ scriptural? Would there ever be such a moment for true believers — a specific time when they would stand before the Lord and experience such a moment, which could only be described as "terror"?

Those questions, my friend, are worth our research. They demand biblical answers, and they are the focus of the thesis of this book.

Rick C. Howard

Rick C. Howard
Redwood City, California
September 1990

Foreword

I was sitting in an open-air transit hall of the Pago Pago Airport in American Samoa, waiting for a flight. It was hot and sticky, typical of the tropics of Polynesia. I leafed through the "to do" file in my travel bag and withdrew the manuscript for Rick Howard's book *The Judgment Seat of Christ*. As I pondered the title, a lump rose in my throat and my heart raced with an excitement that seemed to cut through the muggy tropical heat.

The Judgment Seat of Christ: I have heard Rick speak powerfully on this subject numerous times. It has marked him, and it has marked me. If he never addresses another subject, his life will have been well-spent for the insight and understanding he has brought to this topic. I can picture his tombstone one day appropriately reading: "The Teacher of the Judgment Seat of Christ."

I have known Rick for two decades. In fact, I am an honorary member of his congregation in Redwood City, California. I have been privileged to be co-laborers with him at seminars and conferences around the world. There are a few great teachers who stand out as pillars amongst the Body of Christ internationally. I count Rick as one of those truly great teachers, according to Ephesians chapter 4. He instructs with scholarly diligence, vivid illustrations and timely humor.

Although *The Judgment Seat of Christ* is a masterful example of the excellence of Rick's God-given teaching gift; although I consider him a true friend; although I respect him and have even received the Word of the Lord through him to me directly on more than one occasion — these are not my reasons for writing this foreword.

My true motivation for recommending this book is because it is for me, here and now. It is for the mission I represent, Youth With A Mission. But I believe it is also the message on the heart of God for the Body of Christ at this point in history — for our benefit, strengthening and preparation to meet our Master as well as a motivation for our service here on earth. It is for leaders and laymen alike everywhere — in the pew, on the streets, and in the marketplace.

Just prior to reading the manuscript for this book I experienced a deep, personal refreshing in the Holy Spirit. He drew me to fall more in love with the Lord Jesus. This message on the judgment seat of Christ was what my soul needed *now* — not only to be better prepared to meet my Savior, but to be motivated in a greater, more solid way, to work for Him. As you walk through the pages of this book, as I have done, you will find your heart stirred, your spirit convicted, and your mind challenged. I believe you will be marked, as I have been marked, by the Spirit of God.

Loren Cunningham
Founder and President
Youth With A Mission

The Judgment Seat of Christ

*W*e are expecting God, in the way of His judgments, to visit this earth: we are waiting for Him. What a thought! We know of these coming judgments; we know that there are tens of thousands of professing Christians who live on in carelessness, and who, if no change come, must perish under God's hand. Oh, shall we not do our utmost to warn them, to plead with and for them, if God may have mercy on them! If we feel our want of boldness, want of zeal, want of power, shall we not begin to wait on God more definitely and persistently as a God of judgment, asking Him so to reveal Himself in the judgments that are coming on our very friends, that we may be inspired with a new fear of Him and them, and constrained to speak and pray as never yet. Verily, waiting on God is not meant to be a spiritual self-indulgence. Its object is to let God and His holiness, Christ and the love that died on Calvary, the Spirit and fire that burns in Heaven and came to earth, get possession of us, to warn and rouse men with the message that we are waiting for God in the way of His judgments. O Christian, prove that you really believe in the God of judgment!

—Andrew Murray:
Waiting on God; Daily Messages for a Month

Chapter 1
Judgment Is Not
An Unannounced Exam

You must take terror where you find it. It can come unexpectedly and unannounced, like a near-miss in traffic, or the approach of a hostile thief or mugger. On the other hand, it may come at the end of an anticipated fear, such as a long-dreaded court appearance, or the necessary preparation for a business or tax audit.

The heartbeat may be the same. You may sweat profusely at both. But there is an obvious difference: The one you have prepared for, and the other comes as a total shock.

Nothing in my travels around the world has been so strange to me as the fearful absence of knowledge and discussion among Christians concerning the Judgment Seat of Christ.

Liberty Is Not License

In fact, definite teaching on Christian responsibility in life and work in general seems lacking everywhere. Christian apathy abounds, and laxness in Christian conduct is promoted as though the grace of God, manifested in salvation, includes a general license for sin!

Liberty, however, is not license, nor is the believer's judicial freedom through Calvary freedom from a holy Christian walk or warfare.

It has been my practice, whenever I am with any group of Christians for more than one service, to give at least one

1

message on the Judgment Seat of Christ. Everywhere I have done this, I found the topic either completely unknown or suspended in some vague theological context.

We need to realize what a high privilege it is to know the ways of God. God's children need to know the different methods by which the Father deals with His own. The Word declares:

The Lord executes righteousness and justice for all who are oppressed.

He made known His ways to Moses, His acts to the children of Israel.

The Lord is merciful and gracious, slow to anger, and abounding in mercy.

He will not always strive with us, nor will He keep His anger forever.

He has not dealt with us according to our sins, nor punished us according to our iniquities.

Psalm 103:6-10

Jesus Christ: Savior and Lord

God always rules for the ultimate good and blessing of His chosen ones. He acts ultimately for the honor and glory of His good name. The scripture offers no conflict between Jesus Christ as *Savior* and Jesus Christ as *Lord.*

Neither is there conflict between the believer's completeness of salvation and his responsibility to God. Never try to demand a difference between the marvelous keeping power of God's Spirit and grace versus the believer's judgment at Christ's hand, where he shall receive blame or praise, reward or loss.

Rejoice at Judgment

The subject of God's justice and judgments is scripturally an occasion for rejoicing. Listen to the Psalmist:

Oh, let the nations be glad and sing for joy!

Psalm 67:4

2

Or again:

> **Let the field be joyful...all the trees of the woods will rejoice before the Lord.**
>
> **For He is coming, for He is coming to judge the earth.**
>
> **Psalm 96:12,13**

C. S. Lewis, the noted English academician, wrote in *Reflections on the Psalms*, "We need not therefore be surprised if the Psalms and the Prophets are full of longing for judgment, and regard the announcement that 'judgment' is coming as good news."

Specifically, the Judgment Seat of Christ is not an "unannounced quiz." Profound biblical teachings concerning judgment in general are abundant, as are intensely specific warnings concerning the *bema* judgment for believers.

However, it is only our faithful pursuit of truth that will bring us to this awareness. The scriptures are explicit. The believer can prepare for it, or he can choose to remain blissfully ignorant of the coming proceedings. I know both attitudes.

The Two Basic Judgments

God's basic standard for evaluating believers is well known. Each will receive either reward or loss of reward in one degree or another of these alternatives at the Judgment Seat of Christ. The result for each believer will be degrees of two basic judgments: *reward* or *loss of reward*.

I was blissfully ignorant as I sat one Monday morning at my desk in downtown Memphis, Tennessee. Mondays were always especially busy for a director of Youth for Christ.

There were newspaper ads which had to be completed before deadline, Bible Club plans to be prepared for several schools that week, and last-minute details for our principal media and rally ministries.

Visit From a Baptist

I was hard at work doing these things when I received a telephone call from my favorite board member, an enthusiastic Baptist layman who always moved me by his consistent witness and deep, sincere love for Jesus Christ.

Ed delighted in telling humorous and even vulnerable episodes about his personal pilgrimage to Christ, and he had been an uncompromising friend and support to my ministry.

More than once I had watched this extremely successful businessman weep as he discussed his most recent sharing of Jesus Christ with others. When Ed spoke, I listened.

"I need to see you for a few minutes this morning," he said in a business-like manner.

"Impossible, Ed," I replied. "I'm uncommonly rushed this morning. Perhaps we could meet midweek?"

"No, Rick, it must be now. I'll come down and wait for a break in your schedule." I heard a click. The line was dead. This was something urgent.

So Ed came and sat in my office as I continued with my busywork. Then I heard him ask softly, "Rick, have you ever thought much about the Judgment Seat of Christ?"

I didn't even look up from my papers. I replied tritely, "Oh, I know there'll be one, Ed..."

There was absolute silence. When I finally looked up in curiosity, I saw tears streaming down Ed's face! I felt ashamed; caught and exposed.

"Oh, Ed, forgive me! Obviously you have something to share with me that's far more important than this work!"

A Businessman's Sermon

Grabbing my Bible, I turned my chair so I could sit knee-to-knee with my friend. "Have at it, pal. I think I'm ready."

4

Ed grinned at me and began. That short Southern Baptist layman took almost three hours and walked me through the scriptures on the Judgment Seat of Christ. The subject had recently made a strong impact on him and, genuinely loving me, he wanted me to be warned also.

When he finally finished, Ed put his hand on my shoulder, as always, and prayed a simple, fervent prayer. Then he stood up, hugged me, and was gone.

I was stunned and shaken! I picked up the phone and dialed the extension of the secretary of this Christian organization.

"Verla, I need to go home. Please line up others to do my assignments the next couple of days."

"Are you sick?" she asked, concerned.

"Yes," I replied, "in a way, but I can't talk about it now."

"All right, honey," she replied in a motherly tone. "I'll take care of everything. You go on home."

My car was parked behind the mission. I almost stumbled to it and began to drive the ten miles out Poplar Boulevard toward my small garage apartment in White Station.

Could It Be True?

I was sobbing and praying at the same time. I was genuinely shaken! Twice I turned the car to the curb and waited to gain my composure. I felt naked, exposed, and totally unprepared.

I had already been in the ministry for seven years, and there had been a genuine measure of blessing and release in my ministry. But I had never heard even one message on the Judgment Seat of Christ, let alone studied the truth for myself.

Could what Ed shared be true? I knew salvation was not attained or affected by good works, but our reward and position in heaven would be. Obviously, all Christians would not have the same station in heaven.

5

As I drove and wept, I was suddenly reminded of a dreadful experience in my freshman year of college. I had achieved a high enough grade point average after my first semester to allow me the privilege of "unlimited cuts" for the next semester.

Without that privilege, an automatic grade reduction would begin after three unexcused absences in any class. In my immaturity, I had abused the privilege; particularly in one Bible class which seemed elementary and basic to me.

The Terror of Being Unprepared

One day I sauntered into the classroom following nearly two weeks of absences. I was at least ten minutes early, but every student was in his seat with his notebook open before him. My heart skipped a beat! I slipped into my seat beside a satirical friend.

"What's up, Jim?" I asked, desperately.

He looked amused. "Oh, nothing special, Howard. Just the mid-semester final — that's all."

The shock on my face must have been obvious. "You've got to be kidding!" I exclaimed.

"Oh, no," Jim teased. "We do lots of exciting things around here. You ought to come around more often!"

I felt foolish, unprepared, and immature. The exam had been properly announced; I had simply been careless about my responsibilities.

No Excuses Accepted

When I approached the professor and pleaded for a personal postponement, he answered sternly, "Mr. Howard, I don't approve of this current attendance policy. I can't punish you for missing class, but you are, nonetheless, responsible for everything that goes on here. You must take the exam this morning with your fellow students or receive an automatic failure on this test." I'd rather forget staring at that blank paper.

The sinking feeling I felt in my stomach then was present now, these many years later. As I drove to my apartment, I realized that a far more serious examination was now before me, and I knew nothing about it, either! I was totally unprepared for it, too! How could I have missed it? What specifics had I missed through my carelessness?

Terror in the Presence of the Lord!

I entered the apartment and began almost four days and nights of study on the Judgment Seat of Christ. It led to the night I described at the beginning of this book — a night of terror in the presence of the Lord — but a night which changed my life!

I think it necessary to remind you of the intention behind the doctrine [of judgment], namely, that we should be daily apprehensive of the coming of the Judge. We are to frame our behavior on the assumption that we shall have to give an account to a Judge who is at hand. This is what the prophet meant by his saying about the man who is blessed: For as much as he orders his words with judgment.

—Rufinus: *A Commentary on The Apostles' Creed*

Chapter 2
Let's Set the Stage

There is no question — the scriptures are clear — the child of God, living under grace, shall never come into condemnation or judgment for sin.[1]

The believer's stand before God is on the firm ground that the penalty for all sin — past, present, and future — has been borne by Christ as the perfect Sacrifice and Substitute. How wonderful are Paul's words to the Colossian believers:

> **And you, being dead in your trespasses and the uncircumcision of your flesh, He has made alive together with Him, having forgiven you all trespasses,**
>
> **having wiped out the handwriting of requirements that was against us, which was contrary to us. And He has taken it out of the way, having nailed it to the cross.**
>
> **Colossians 2:13,14**

Most scholars agree that this "handwriting" was a publicly displayed statement of indebtedness or legal obligation. Such a list of broken laws was often nailed to the prisoner's jail door as justification for his sentence.

Christ removed the indictments from us and nailed them to His own cross! He also nailed the Mosaic law, with all its decrees, to His cross, paying in His death for the failure and the sinfulness of man.

The Believer's Security

The true believer in Jesus Christ is not only placed beyond condemnation; he is placed "in Christ," and is accepted in the perfection of Christ![2] He is loved by God as Christ is loved.

9

Salvation and justification are complete in simple faith. The original language of Colossians 2:14 in the original Greek translates, "...taken it [sin] out of the way." This is actually a strong expression for putting something out of sight completely.

Jesus Himself made any other understanding impossible when He said, "He who believes in Him [God's Son] is not condemned..." (John 3:18). The believer is secure in Christ Jesus! Praise God for such unbounded love and grace.

"Well, then," you say, "*that* settles it. What's all this talk of terror?"

Jesus As Lord

Quite simple, actually — and dangerously overlooked. The fact is, Jesus Christ is not only our *Savior* — the perfect and complete Substitute and Sacrifice for sin — He is also our *Lord.*

The original creed of the Christian faith is: Jesus Christ is Lord! The simplest and clearest "formula" for becoming a Christian is given this way in scripture: "that if you confess with your mouth the Lord Jesus and believe in your heart that God has raised Him from the dead, you will be saved" (Romans 10:9).

The word "Lord" — *kurios* in the original Greek — is ultimately more a position than a name. "Lord" is the one to whom you yield complete control. *Kurios* is related to our words "despot" or "dictator."

The Redeemer Expects Results

The clear concept of salvation, particularly in its explanation of redemption, is that we are bought back, or freed, *in order to be used.* We are returned to a state of value and fruitfulness. The Redeemer expects results, for He is not only our Savior; He is our Lord.

Dr. C. S. Lovett writes, "He has given every Christian a job. Those ignoring His orders will feel awful when He appears."

The Apostle John warned, "And now, little children, abide in Him, that when He appears, we may have confidence and not be ashamed before Him at His coming" (1 John 2:28).

Unfaithful, Fruitless Servants

This is a clear reference to the Second Coming of Christ. The original language speaks of a slave who has an open or good conscience before his master, compared with the cringing, terror, and shame experienced by a faithless servant.

In the Gospel of John, Jesus explains that "He who abides in Me, and I in Him, bears much fruit..." (John 15:5). When Christ appears *as Lord,* many servants will "shrink back from Him in shame," for they have been unfaithful servants. They are, in other words, unfruitful.

Paul's Advice to Servants

Paul addresses the general issues of Christian submission and relationships in two parallel passages: Colossians 3 and Ephesians 6. He speaks concerning families, government, and employment. And he addresses these words specifically to servants in Ephesians 6:

Servants, be obedient to those who are your masters according to the flesh, with fear and trembling, in sincerity of heart, as to Christ;

not with eye service, as men-pleasers, but as servants of Christ, doing the will of God from the heart,

with good will doing service, as to the Lord, and not to men,

knowing that whatever good anyone does, he will receive the same from the Lord, whether he is a slave or free.

And you, masters, do the same things to them, giving up threatening, knowing that your own Master also is in heaven, and there is no partiality with Him.

Ephesians 6:5-9

And to the Colossians Paul writes these words, adding an important phrase from what he wrote to the Ephesians.

Servants, obey in all things your masters according to the flesh, not with eye service, as men-pleasers, but in sincerity of heart, fearing God.

And whatsoever you do, do it heartily, as to the Lord and not to men,

knowing that from the Lord you will receive the reward of the inheritance; for you serve the Lord Christ.

But he who does wrong will be repaid for the wrong which he has done, and there is no partiality.

Masters, give your servants what is just and fair, knowing that you also have a Master in heaven.

Colossians 3:22-4:1

Good and Bad News

Notice particularly the issues in these scriptures of *motive, reward, service to Christ,* and *compensation.* They are expressed in the idea, "You shall receive what you have done." That's both good and bad news for any servant or believer.

When believers stand at the Judgment Seat of Christ at His coming, they will be judged according to their works; according to the fruitfulness of their lives. This judgment will in no way reflect on whether they are saved or lost.

The Judgment Seat of Christ determines the reward or loss of reward for the service of each believer. Those standing at the Judgment Seat of Christ are not only saved and safe; they will already be in heaven!

Grace and Works

They will certainly not be there on the basis of their *merits* or *works,* but on the much more certain ground of God's divine *grace,* which was made possible through the sacrifice of Jesus Christ.

Grace is free, but works are not — and free grace is not cheap. We are born again to have purpose and be useful. God expects certain things from you after you become a Christian. In other words, your Christian life is going somewhere!

We are "...created in Christ Jesus for good works, which God prepared beforehand that we should walk in them" (Ephesians 2:10).

The Judgment Seat

The word "judgment" in the term "the Judgment Seat of Christ" is the Greek word *bema*, or *bematos*, which refers to a raised platform of arbitration and reward. This term is used ten times in the New Testament.

The *bema* is never a judicial bench; instead, it is a place of *inspection, oration,* and *performance.* Like the platform at a county fair or a beauty contest, it is a place where the believer's life and works are examined.

Understanding God's Justice

Here, overcomers are rewarded, and unfaithful servants will suffer loss. *To understand the Judgment Seat of Christ is to understand the justice of God.*

A young student wrote me:

When I began researching the Judgment Seat, I grasped a reality of the justice of God. I had never seen that before. There were times when I would feel the seriousness and heaviness of my spirit as I understood what was in store for the Christian. There were times when I felt it in such a strong way that I could not take a full breath of air, because my insides seemed to be knotted up — much like when you're so tense and nervous that it's difficult to breathe!

No wonder Paul wrote concerning this judgment, "Knowing, therefore, the terror of the Lord, we persuade men..." (2 Corinthians 5:11).

[1]John 3:18; 5:24; 6:37; Romans 5:1; 8:1; First Corinthians 11:32.

[2]First Corinthians 1:30; Ephesians 1:6; Colossians 2:10; Hebrews 10:14.

It was said by Coleridge that our greatest mission is to rescue admitted truths from the neglect caused by their universal admission.

—F. B. Meyer: *Joseph*

Chapter 3
The Place and the Issue

"Take the exam," my instructor had firmly admonished, "or accept an automatic failure." Those words remind me of remarkably similar words found in scripture:

> But why do you judge your brother? Or why do you show contempt for your brother? For we shall all stand before the judgment seat of Christ.
>
> For it is written: "As I live, says the Lord, every knee shall bow to Me, and every tongue shall confess to God."
>
> So then each of us shall give account of himself to God.
>
> **Romans 14:10-12**

This is one of the ten New Testament locations where the word *bema* is used, and it is one of two specific places in the Word of God where the term "Judgment Seat of Christ" is used.

Exclusion and Inclusion

Observe that the Apostle Paul uses the personal pronoun of family language, "we." Only Christians are referred to this way. This is both an exclusion (of sinners) and an important inclusion (of believers).

The word "shall" denotes divine certainty. Earlier, Paul had said, "...we are chastened by the Lord, that we may not be condemned with the world" (1 Corinthians 11:32).

It is also worthy to note the word "all." There are no exceptions! Every believer — including the apostle, the Christians to whom he wrote at Rome, and all others of the household of faith, including you and me — will be there: "We shall *all* stand before the judgment seat of Christ."

As Dr. L. Sale-Harrison wrote many years ago in a book on this subject, "Whatever this judgment seat is, we shall all stand before it. This scripture admits of no question at this point."

Our Future Hope

The other specific reference to this judgment is in Second Corinthians 5. This is a phenomenal chapter of future hope and believer's purpose, especially concerning the resurrection of the believer's body.

In this context, the apostle compares the realities of present sufferings to the coming "weight of glory." He speaks of a moment when we will receive a new body, "...a house not made with hands, eternal in the heavens" (v. 1).

It is by faith we walk, he says, confident that to be absent from the body is to be present with the Lord (v. 8).

"Knowing the Terror"

Therefore we make it our aim, whether present or absent, to be well pleasing to Him.

For we must all appear before the judgment seat of Christ, that each one may receive the things done in the body, whether good or bad.

Knowing, therefore, the terror of the Lord, we persuade men; but we are well known to God, and I trust are well known to our consciences.

2 Corinthians 5:9-11

In this passage, we see that Paul again uses the word "we," addressing it to believers. It is interesting that such personal pronouns occur more than thirty times in this relatively short chapter.

Also note the words "must" and "all" in the passage. In verse 10, Paul writes, "we must all appear," and in Romans 14:10 he says, "we shall all stand."

Revealed by Fire

"Appear" is a translation for the Greek word *phonero*, which means "to be clearly seen, to be explicitly manifested or discerned." This same word is used in First Corinthians 3:13, an important passage we will examine in detail later. That passage warns that "each one's work will become *manifest*; for the Day will declare it, because it will be revealed by fire...."

You can see, then, that both the believer *and* his work shall obviously be revealed at the Judgment Seat of Christ.

Note also the contrast in Second Corinthians 5:10 ("each one may receive the things done in the body") to Romans 14:12 ("each of us shall give account of himself to God"). Although these phrases are similar, they reveal different *activities* that will take place at this moment of review before the Judgment Seat.

Privilege and Mandate

It can be said that the use of the word "may" in the passage from Second Corinthians suggests that this judgment is both a *privilege* as well as a *mandate*. The Judgment Seat of Christ will be a time of clarification and explanation.

Jesus contrasted "the unrighteous judge" with the believer's hope of a righteous hearing of his case before the Judgment Seat of the Lord. "Yea, in the way of thy judgments, O Lord, have we waited for thee," declares Isaiah 26:8 *(King James Version)*.

Andrew Murray writes in "The Gracious Judge," from *Daily Messages for a Month:*

> Judgment prepares the way, and breaks out in wonderful mercy. It is written: "Thou shalt be redeemed with judgment." Wait on God, in the faith that His tender mercy is working out His redemption in the midst of judgment. Wait on Him, He will be gracious to you.

The Strongest Word for Fear

Note the apostle's concluding statement in Second Corinthians 5:11, "Knowing, therefore, the terror of the Lord, we persuade men."

Here is the strongest Greek word for "fear" that we might use: *phobia*. One writer remarked, "This is the fear excited by the thought of standing before the judgment seat of Christ and having one's whole life exposed and estimated."[1]

Remember John's words: "And now, little children, abide in Him, that when He appears, we may have confidence and not be ashamed before Him at His coming" (1 John 2:28). Some translators suggest that in place of "ashamed before Him," the stronger phrase, "shrink back in terror from Him at His coming" should be used.

The Judgment Seat of Christ is not going to be a tea party or a Sunday School picnic; rather, it will be a moment to be known by its *terror*. Knowing this coming terror, every sincere teacher attempts to persuade his brethren of it, like Paul persuaded the Early Church and like Ed persuaded me.

"Will I ever fear my Savior?" you ask. "Doesn't perfect love cast out fear? Jesus is my loving Friend, and God is my Father. I can't imagine being before them in an attitude of terror."

I'm convinced the answer to such genuinely perceived Christian confidence is found in the roles we assign Christ. We choose to know our Christ only as Intercessor, Redeemer, and Friend of sinners. But He is also Lord and Master, Ruler of all nature, and coming King and Judge!

Knowing Only One Side of the Father

Imagine a young man growing up in a fine, upper middle-class home, where his father not only adequately provides for him, but personally befriends him. They golf and sail together, go camping, and frequently have long, intimate, and vulnerable conversations. It is the happiest of relationships possible between a father and his son.

One sad day, this son, having gotten in with the wrong crowd, joins his worthless companions in committing a crime. They are arrested by the police, and soon find themselves standing before the bar of justice.

The bailiff calls out the number of the court and announces the name of the judge. Everyone in the courtroom stands in respect as the black-robed figure enters the room.

The three young defendants stand before the bench in fear and apprehension. The young son knows the physical figure of the man so well, but he has never seen him as he is today; he has never known him in this role. It is indeed his father, but now he is also his judge!

Another Portrait of Christ

Revelation 1:13-16 gives us a picture of Christ that most Christians have never considered:

...clothed with a garment down to the feet and girded about the chest with a golden band.

His head and His hair were white like wool, as white as snow, and His eyes like a flame of fire;

His feet were like fine brass, as if refined in a furnace, and His voice as the sound of many waters:

He had in His right hand seven stars, out of His mouth went a sharp two-edged sword, and His countenance was like the sound of many waters.

That is hardly a typical Sunday School picture of Jesus Christ! Incidentally, the "garment down to the feet" is the Greek word *poderes*, most often used for the robe of the judge or judge-priest.

No wonder the response of the Apostle John to this vision was to fall at His feet as dead! Jesus Christ is Lord. It is He with whom we have to do. *He who has redeemed and loved us must also examine and judge us!*

---

[1]Alfred Plummer, *Critical and Exegetical Commentary on the Second Epistle of St. Paul to the Corinthians.*

*A*t every turn of your life, keep the end in view; remember that you will have to stand before a strict Judge, who knows everything, who cannot be won over by gifts or talked around by excuses, who will give you your desserts. What sort of defense will you make before One who knows the worst that can be said against you — poor, sinful fool, so often panic-stricken when you meet with human disapproval! Strange, that you should look forward so little to the Day of Judgment, when there will be no counsel to plead for you, because everyone will be hard put to it to maintain his own cause! Now is the time to work, while there is a harvest to be reaped, now is the time when tears and sighs and lamenting of yours will be taken into account, and listened to, and can make satisfaction for the debt you owe.

—Thomas à Kempis: *Imitation of Christ*

Chapter 4
The Vision

Isaw the redeemed of all ages, like the endless waving of grain in a Kansas wheat field.

My rearing had always been in small Christian groups. Christianity had always been perceived by me as a minority experience. I had no preparation for the endless multitudes of white-robed throngs of believers.

I remembered a moment, standing on the deck of the old Cunard liner, *Queen Mary*, in mid-Atlantic. The limitlessness of the surrounding ocean was like the limitlessness of the gathered Church that I saw in this moment. All Christians of every age were there.

The Sounds of Sobbing and Rejoicing

What came next was not a sight, but a sound. I heard two contrasting and clashing noises. One appeared to be the sound of weeping. It was the guttural sobbing of lost life which I had mentally reserved long ago as a sound-picture of the damned. Yet I knew instinctively that there were no lost here. This was the gathered redeemed, and no one would be unsaved from this moment on.

In contrast, there was the sound of rejoicing, like a thousand camp meetings rolled into one, or the gathering of a multitude of choirs in a gala "Hallelujah Chorus." What release! What praise! And by infinite comparison, what contrast: the deepest sound of uncontrollable weeping and unrestrained joy of released praise.

21

The sounds clashed like great opposing cymbals: weeping and rejoicing — praise and sorrow — success and failure — loss and reward.

For some reason, my eyes were drawn to a group of Christians to my right. There was a figure among them I knew to be the Christ. From the distance, I only felt His identity, for the vision was not clear.

His Torch Is in His Hand

I did see, however, that He carried a torch of fire in His hand. It was a torch not unlike the kind carried by runners in the world's Olympic games. He seemed to be speaking briefly to every Christian.

The conversation was then followed by dropping the torch to a pile of stubble and grass in front of each believer's feet. There was a fire and then a response.

Stubble? My eyes immediately fell to my own feet. I knew the meaning of that symbol: that which was dissolvable — the burnable — the loss.

My deepest fears were realized. At my feet was a pile of consumable wood, grass, and hay like a raked-up stack after I had cut and raked my lawn.

I felt sweat on the palms of my hands, and I remember crying out, more to myself than to anyone around, "O God, is this all I have to show for seven years of ministry? Have my motives and my work been so impure?"

Immediately, in the spirit, I heard these words: "Son, look around."

I quickly apprised myself of the fact that every believer I could see had a similar stack at his feet. Admittedly, some were smaller and others larger than the one at my feet, but I saw no one without such a stack.

Just as clearly, I heard the Spirit say, "And only, son, when all the dross is burned, will it be revealed what remains. *Wait for the fire.*"

From that moment, I felt free to turn my thoughts away from the fearful stack of worthless works at my feet. I was standing in a small, familiar band of people whom I knew. My father, a minister of the Gospel until his death in his mid-eighties, was among the group.

My Spiritual Mentor

My primary attention was drawn across the circle to a face and form as familiar as any I have ever known. It was the diminutive Englishwoman who, with her husband, had been so supportive in the small Holiness congregation in Sharon, Pennsylvania, where I had been reared.

She and her husband had always sat in the front row at every service. For many years she had led our congregation in a monthly missionary service which had greatly influenced my life. Furthermore, she had taught me as a primary student in the plain, basement Sunday School class of that church.

Since my birth had come later in the life of my parents, my natural grandparents were all deceased. So she had always been "Grandmother Shipton" to me. There had been an unusual bonding in our lives.

When I became a difficult and rebellious teenager, and drifted from spiritual priorities, she would come up to me, putting her small hand on my shoulder, and say, "Ricky, son, I'm praying for you. God has a great purpose for your life."

I would politely shake her hand from my shoulder and say with amusement, "Don't you pray for me, Grandma Shipton!" At that time, I couldn't have meant it more. I knew God answered her prayers, and that was the last thing I wanted at that moment!

That godly saint, whose focus was heaven, and whose love of Jesus was as transparent as life itself, was consistently faithful to intercession and purpose.

My Rebellion Ends

One Sunday night during my years of rebellion, I was sitting in my customary place, the rear pew, with some other teenagers. We had passed pictures and notes during my father's sermon. When I stood for the altar call, with head bowed and eyes closed, my hands gripping the back of the pew in front of me, I instinctively knew Grandma Shipton was coming after me!

I didn't hear footsteps, because she couldn't have weighed ninety pounds. Nor had I ever known her to approach someone personally in that way before or after. But I knew she was coming, and soon I felt her hand on my shoulder. It was accompanied not by a request, but by a command — a command backed by fourteen years of prayer.

"Son," she said, "it's time."

I broke like a little child as she led me to the altar and to a place of repentance and full surrender to the Lordship of Jesus Christ.

"Well Done, Thou Good and Faithful Servant"

"Lily Shipton!"

The voice, like the sound of many waters, startled my reverie.

Jesus was standing before my mentor in the spirit. I don't think I had ever heard her first name; certainly not that I remembered. She was always "Grandma Shipton" to me.

"Lily Shipton," Jesus spoke again. "Well done, thou good and faithful servant."

I saw His hand drop the torch to the top of grass and stubble piled at her feet. It burned instantly, like a flash of light, and my eyes could only see a goodly pile of gold and silver pieces as well as precious jewels lying scattered at her feet.

I saw her bend over, reaching to gather the valuables. Taking them in her hands, she laid them at Jesus' feet, and I heard her begin to praise the Lord. How I remember that spirit of praise: "I love You, Jesus! I love You, Jesus!" she cried.

As I heard her rejoice, I was reminded by the Lord of the last time I had seen her on the earth.

A Word From Eternity

I had returned to my parents' home for a Christmas vacation. My ministry had taken me to live in a region far from Pennsylvania, and I had barely kept in touch with the old home church.

Grandma Shipton was now in her nineties, and was partially blind. In the last year, she had become quite senile, my dad had written me, and often she could not remember or recognize him when he visited her, even though he had been her pastor for almost thirty years.

During my vacation, Dad had said, "Son, I think you should come with me today to visit Grandma Shipton. It's probably the last time you'll see her alive."

I had reluctantly accompanied him. I felt no purpose could be served to see her in her present condition, but any chance to spend time with my dad was always a privilege.

We arrived at the simple, two-story frame house. Grandma's daughter, Ione, met us at the door. Every morning she dressed her mother, sat her in the darkened living room in her favorite rocking chair, with her shawl across her shoulders, and the old, worn Bible on her lap.

Ione reminded me that Grandma now seldom recognized even her closest family, but she thanked me nonetheless for coming.

While Dad and Ione talked in the entry, I started to enter the living room through the open hall. Suddenly I heard her voice. Grandma Shipton was speaking! Because of her condition, it sounded like a word from eternity.

"Ricky, son, is that you? Ricky, I pray for you every day. God has a great work for you to do."

I was startled. Was I hearing things? No, Dad and Ione stood behind me, looks of shock on their faces. They had heard her, too!

She didn't speak another sensible word in the hour that followed. Her conversation was fragile and fragmented, rambling and disconnected. God had allowed her spirit one clear, unrepeatable moment. She was irrevocably bonded to that little boy by vision and through prayer. What a word that was to me then and even is to this day.

"Ricky, son, I pray for you every day. God has a great work for you to do."

Our difficulty at the judgment seat of Christ will not be with passports, but with baggage. That is the way it usually is when one travels.

—Dr. Pietsch, speaker at a Moody Institute Founder's Week

Chapter 5
What Lies at Our Feet

When my friend Ed had warned me of the Judgment Seat of Christ, I was driven by conscience to my apartment to begin four days of reading and research.

One particular passage of scripture became dominant in my thinking. I suppose I read First Corinthians 3 at least fourteen times between Monday and Thursday!

That passage, in my estimation, gives power and drama to the biblical teaching on the Judgment Seat of Christ.

The context of First Corinthians 3 is undoubtedly *collective*; that is, it concerns the Church in Corinth, and is specifically directed to Christian co-workers who had helped lay the foundation and build the Christian community in Corinth.

The Individual's Responsibility

But one can also find everywhere in the passage the responsibility of the *individual*. It can be said that Paul is addressing Christian ministers — his co-workers — on the general subject of *every* believer's appearance at the Judgment Seat of Christ.

The carnality and immaturity of the Corinthian believers provides the background for this teaching. The sign of their immaturity was their division over different teachings about diet.

Milk vs. Meat

In typical Pauline fashion, Paul chided these believers for existing on *"milk"* — that which had passed through

29

another's digestive system; i.e., foundational, "ABC teaching" — as opposed to *"meat"* — that which they personally studied, apprehended, and applied.

Although the newborn are to seek the unadulterated milk of the Word, continued dependence on it leaves a believer unskilled, undiscerning, and unfruitful, according to Hebrews 5:11-14.

Such immaturity, in fact, is even dangerous for continuing faith, according to Hebrews 6, because a person depending on milk always builds his Christian life around the source of earthly teachers.

The True Foundation

The true foundation for all Christian life, according to First Corinthians 3:11, is Jesus Christ. All believers, including teachers and individual Christians, build upon *that* foundation. Let us see this in the Word itself:

> For no other foundation can anyone lay than that which is laid, which is Jesus Christ.
>
> Now if anyone builds on this foundation with gold, silver, precious stones, wood, hay, straw,
>
> each one's work will become manifest; for the Day will declare it, because it will be revealed by fire; and the fire will test each one's work, of what sort it is.
>
> If anyone's work which he has built on it endures, he will receive a reward.
>
> If anyone's work is burned, he will suffer loss; but he himself will be saved, yet so as through fire.
>
> Do you not know that you are the temple of God and that the Spirit of God dwells in you?
>
> If anyone defiles the temple of God, God will destroy him. For the temple of God is holy, which temple you are.
>
> 1 Corinthians 3:11-17

A continuing discussion on whether "you" in this passage refers to the Corinthian church collectively or to individuals is fruitless. The overall teaching of scripture is clear that both are applicable.

All individuals build their personal lives upon the foundation of Jesus Christ, just as all pastors or teachers build upon the previously laid foundation of the apostles and the prophets!

At Issue: "The Day"

The ultimate issue of First Corinthians 3 is *"the* Day" or *that* day. Paul further reveals this in the following chapter. Here, he compares the Judgment Seat of Christ to both the judgment of his life made by fellow believers and judgment he had received from human courts ("the day of man"). He had faced both in his personal life and ministry.

He writes in chapter 4:

> **But with me it is a very small thing that I should be judged by you or by a human court. In fact, I do not even judge myself.**
>
> **For I know nothing against myself, yet I am not justified by this; but He who judges me is the Lord.**
>
> **Therefore judge nothing before the time, until the Lord comes, who will both bring to light the hidden things of darkness and reveal the counsels of the hearts; and then each one's praise will come from God.**

1 Corinthians 4:3-5

We have already established beyond question that all of the redeemed from throughout the ages will stand together at the Judgment Seat of Christ.

Motives Will Be Revealed

We are all there. Christ is the Judge there. But along with us and Christ, our *works* will be there — the fruit of our life.

In the image of First Corinthians 3, our work may be in the form of wood, hay, and stubble — that which has been of the flesh and pride; that which was carried out with wrong motives or done to the tune of carnal disuse.

But it also may be there in the form of gold, silver, and precious stones, representing that which has been good, obedient, sacrificial, and done out of pure motives.

Our every action, motive, and work done upon earth will be there to be judged.

The phrase in Second Corinthians 5:10, "each one may receive the things done in the body," actually refers to the things done *through* the body, or while we were in our physical body.

Believers on Probation

From the time of our conversion to Christ, a believer is in a probationary period — a time of test and of opportunity.

Grace, love, and mercy must always be balanced by justice. We have been extended grace, but the Judgment Seat of Christ is a time of *justice.* One student commented, "Grace gets you to the judgment seat, but justice will burn everything that grace covered."

We see this in the life of Joseph. The scripture records, "Until the time that his word came to pass, the Word of the Lord tested him" (Psalm 105:19).

We also see it in the life of Abraham. In Nehemiah, the Levites said concerning Abraham:

> **You are the Lord God, who chose Abram, and brought him out of Ur of the Chaldees, and gave him the name Abraham;**
>
> *You found his heart faithful before You,* **and made a covenant with him... You have performed Your words, for You are righteous.**
>
> **Nehemiah 9:7,8**

In both scriptures, the word for "tested" or "found to be faithful" is the Greek word *eurisko* — "to discover by inquiring, or to prove," and in the Hebrew it is *matza* — "to cause to come forth."

Life: Our Tremendous Opportunity

While the believer is in the physical body, his or her entire experience is, in a sense, a test. The believer's life in the body is a tremendous opportunity for growth, fruitfulness and, above all, conformity to the likeness of Jesus Christ. (See Ephesians 1:4; Romans 8:28,29.)

Properly lived, this life itself is a wonderful act of worship which brings praise to the glory of God's grace. This life is also the believer's only arena to establish the way he will spend eternity. This is the clear teaching of Romans 14:10-12: "...so then each of us shall give account of himself to God" (v. 12).

A Fearful Accounting

The large pile of straw, wood, and stubble I saw at my feet was alarming and startling. I knew it was a symbolic representation of the summation of my life and ministry! How well I remember crying out, "O God, is this all I have to show for seven years of ministry?"

An accounting is always frightening. Who doesn't feel a tingle of fear when he sends in a tax report, take a driver's test, or hand in an essay examination to an instructor? It's the best we have or can do under the circumstances, but how will it be evaluated? "Each of us shall give account of himself to God."

As I was involved in my intense, four-day study, these words reminded me to something. I smiled to myself when I finally remembered. Those were the words my father frequently said to me as a teenager. "Richard," he would say (I was always Ricky until such a moment of judgment!) — "Richard, give account of yourself!"

I knew what he meant: "Where were you? Who were you? What did you do?" I would never have lied to my father, but I often thought he didn't need to know all the details! The older I became, however, the more I came to understand his concern, and the more wisdom I saw in throwing myself on the mercy of his court!

Squandered Potential

Leonard Ravenhill wrote concerning the Judgment Seat of Christ, "God is not going to measure your intellect or ministry. He is going to try your life with fire."

"To give an account" means to report and answer for our opportunities. *"Loss" to a believer will be the realization of squandered potential.*

The Justice ruling at Christ's judgment seat will set the tone or measure of eternity, because that day will disclose or declare our faithfulness, our life, and our work.

The Judgment Seat of Christ is the posting of the exam grades, the evaluation of our life's choices, and the establishment of our position for eternity.

Dr. C. S. Lovett has written in *Christian Workers Service Bureau Magazine*: "Blood washed believers will be spotless in God's sight, but not all will have the same service record. God is after obedience. In fact, He says the Christian's love is measured by obedience (John 14:21). Salvation gets us to heaven, but works determine what we do after we get there."

A Need for Mercy

I shall never forget a spring evening in 1956. I was a high school student who had just begun to drive an automobile. My father had recently purchased only the second new car of his life, a 1955 Chevrolet sports coupe with a black front, white top and back, and beautiful white vinyl interior. It was a beaut! (Dad was almost ashamed to drive the car in funerals.) Everyone knew I had picked out the car.

The evening came when I was finally given permission to drive the car unaccompanied on a date. My girl friend sat up front, and my best friend and his girl sat in the back seat. We were so proud driving through town! The car seemed as wide as a boat. I drove extremely carefully.

At the end of the evening, I took my girl friend home first. She lived down a long, private lane. I parked carefully, walked her to the front door, and did the expected amenities.

When I returned, my friends had moved to the front seat, so we were three across. I put the car in reverse, not knowing that the front door on the passenger side had been left partially open. The driveway was narrow, and a tree caught the partially opened door, cramming it into the front fender!

I can still feel that "crunch" in my stomach these many years later. I knew when I got home, Dad would say, "Richard, give account of yourself." I would have to answer, "Dad, do you remember the design of our car on the right-hand side? Well, I've added a wrinkle of my own!"

Each one of us shall give account of himself. My family's car was its only valuable, owned possession. I was returning it worth *less* than when it had been entrusted to me. Not willfully, but carelessly I had misused my privilege. Such will be the eternal story of many believers.

"If anyone's work is burned, he will suffer loss...."

You hear of a book of the living, and a book of those who are not being saved. There we shall all be inscribed or rather have been inscribed already, according to the desserts of each man's life on this earth. Wealth has no advantage: nor is justice corrupted, as here, by favor or hatred or any other such influence. We have all been entered in the book by God's finger, and that book will be opened in the day of revelation.

—Gregory of Nazianzus: *By God's Finger*

Chapter 6
What Is the Nature of Works?

C hristianity is the world's only religion that sets a man right by grace and simple faith and then supernaturally empowers his life and enables his works. Then — wonder of wonders — that man is *rewarded* for the works which he had nothing to do with in the first place! What a wonder is God's grace!

When you visit the archaeological site of ancient Corinth in Greece, you can see the *bema* stone that the archaeologists unearthed. It was doubtless at that very place where proconsul Gallio arbitrated the issue which the Jews brought against Paul.

The Bible records, "...the Jews with one accord rose up against Paul and brought him to the judgment seat..." (Acts 18:12). After Gallio rendered a favorable decision for Paul, it says, "...he drove them from the judgment seat" (Acts 18:16).

Remember that *bema* means "raised platform," and could even represent the front platform of a church or hall. In the ancient world, the raised platform was often where the president or the umpire of the Grecian games would sit. From there he would watch the events, and from there he would ultimately reward the winners.

A Place of Inspection and Reward

The *bema* was never a judicial bench; instead, it was a seat of evaluation, arbitration and, most often, reward. Certainly the Judgment Seat of Christ is not a place of condemnation, for Romans 8:1 states, "There is therefore now no condemnation to those who are in Christ Jesus...." The Judgment Seat of Christ is, rather, a moment of inspection and an opportunity for reward.

What, then, is the nature of these works that are being inspected? Why would Paul use the terms "gold, silver, precious stones, wood, hay, straw," and so forth as a graphic illustration of persuasion?

As other writers have suggested, this may be biblical symbolism. Gold is an almost universal symbol for divinity and God's righteousness, as declared in Jesus Christ.[1] The Word of God is clear that it is "the righteousness of God" which we must possess; "even the righteousness of God which is through faith in Jesus Christ to all and on all who believe" (Romans 3:22).

Similarly, silver is often connected with redemption and its unique price.[2] And precious stones, or "jewels," are often connected in the Bible with the value of God's people to the Lord.

Such is certainly true in a study of the High Priest's breastplate. It is clearly stated in the prophecy of Malachi:

> **"They shall be Mine, says the Lord of hosts, "on the-day that I make them My jewels."**

> **Malachi 3:17**

L. Sale-Harrison was led to remark on this passage:

> We are therefore warranted in stating the successful builder in his life, walk, and testimony, is revealing the glory and beauty of the Lord. Such a believer has only one person he desires to please — "his Lord," and one thing alone to preach, "God's Word." This faithful soul continually glorifies in his Lord and increasingly revels in His word.[3]

However, as meaningful as such a study would be, the clear meaning of Paul in First Corinthians 3 is permanence versus impermanence — that which will remain after being exposed to the fire of Christ's judgment!

Expensive Building Materials

The precious or valuable stones mentioned probably refer to the use of better and more expensive building materials, such as granite and marble, as opposed to straw and grass. The latter were often used with wooden or common homes and to thatch the roofs of peasant homes.

At issue, then, is the priority of design, the durability of the building materials, *and* the care and skillfulness of the craftsman. Even the craftsman's attitude will be judged: What did he build, and how did he build upon the irreplaceable foundation of Jesus Christ as Lord?

Wood, hay, and stubble may make a bigger display and larger bulk, but exposed to fire they are quickly burned! The original Greek language is specific. It uses the definite article "that day," meaning that specific day, well known to believers, will quickly clarify any remaining questions. Everything will be made clear, visible, and plain then.

Is Heaven Its Own Reward?

You may ask, "But of what ultimate concern can that be to a believer? Won't it be enough to make it in? Won't heaven be its own reward?"

The answer to such a question is, of course, relative. Yes, indeed, heaven is better than the alternative! Only those who are redeemed are at the Judgment Seat of Christ. There will be no question of saved or not saved there. The Judgment Seat of Christ is clearly distinguished from the Great White Throne Judgment, at which the rest of mankind will stand.

The worst scenario which Paul can imagine is:

> **If anyone's work is burned, he will suffer loss; but he himself will be saved, *yet so as through fire.***

> **1 Corinthians 3:15**

The word "burned" is future passive: "to burn up completely." And the phrase "yet so as through fire" has been explained by scholars to mean, "as one who dashes through the flames safely, but with the smell of fire upon him."

Earlier I described the cacophony of sound which I heard in my vision. One of the contrasting sounds was the weeping and wailing I had previously reserved in my mind for the lost.

The Fire of Exposure

At the Judgment Seat of Christ, nothing will be hidden. The fire of exposure will test every servant's life. When the Christian has built adequately, and his labor stands the test, he will receive a reward. But, oh, the loss to those believers who have been unfaithful in service, or unholy in life!

It is possible to be truly born again, yet be consistently unfaithful and disobedient, thus dishonoring the Lord in conduct and life's work.

Can you imagine the seriousness of this truth? Is it possible for you to imagine what it would be like to find all our work — that which we professed to be done for Christ — consumed, shot through by light, figuratively going up in smoke?

So many things believers boast of in this life have been for self, not for Christ! No wonder John speaks of shame, or shrinking from the Lord in terror!

The sacrifice of Christ on the cross, the marvelous grace of God, the victorious company of fellow believers who have sacrificed in faithfulness — these will all haunt us in that moment. Nothing will be missed in God's fire. "For our God is a consuming fire" (Hebrews 12:29).

My Significant Friend

When I stood at the Judgment Seat of Christ, I stood in the company of particularly important and significant "others" in my Christian experience.

Immediately to my left was a young man I had gone to school with seven years before. Although he was a college sophomore and I was a mere high school sophomore at that time, we had been very close through our mutual spiritual commitment.

During the same Spiritual Emphasis Week, he and I had surrendered to the call of God to full-time Christian ministry. From that time forward, we frequently met for prayer and study. What a contrast we were! He was tall and handsome, a student leader in every field. I was still an under-developed early adolescent. Yet we were bonded, and I knew instinctively why he stood there with me at this vision of Christ's judgment seat.

I am not a "Daddy-called preacher." Raised in a minister's home in the toughest of circumstances, I had no desire to repeat the experience! From my earliest commitment, I had both loved Jesus and run from His call upon my life.

My call to the ministry was a wrestling with God, like Jacob, which left me marked and broken. If there had been any place to run — any way to resign and keep the freedom of full experience in Christ Jesus — I would have found it! (The will of God is often not choice, but full surrender.)

A Call Is Compromised

How well I remember a spring evening in Georgia, sitting with my friend in the front seat of his car. He had just announced his engagement to a beautiful coed whom I knew would compromise the call of God on his life.

I begged and pleaded with him, sobbing as only a young adolescent male has freedom to do. He placed his hand on my shoulder and said, as a big brother would, "It's all right, Ricky. I know what I'm doing. Don't worry, friend."

Those words still follow me today! They are certainly the feeling of many Christians: "Don't worry. I know what I'm doing."

In the corner of my eye, I saw the majestic Christ approach my friend. He was carrying that flaming torch that was spitting sparks out of its intensity! Christ called him by a nickname known only to friends like me, and He lowered the torch to the pile of grass and stubble at my friend's feet.

Suddenly all was burned! Nothing remained but a blackened circle of earth. My friend covered his face with his empty hands and began to weep. I have no words for what I saw and felt. What tragedy! What loss! This is an irrevocable and unchangeable verdict!

If anyone's work is burned, he will suffer loss....

---

[1]The Mosaic Tabernacle is a particular study in this, as are many related scriptures: Psalm 20:9,10 Proverbs 16:16; 1 Peter 1:7

[2]See Exdus 30:12-16 and compare with 1 Peter 1:18,19.

[3]L. Sale-Harrison in *The Judgment Seat of Christ*

*C*hristian life will yield up its secret to examination and will be revealed as love. "At evening we shall be judged by Love," and Love will judge our deeds and character, omissions and motives. In the light of eternity the Christian vocation will be understood as what it is: a vocation to love which affects the growth of man to maturity. Law and love will be seen in their original unity. The revelation of God concerning Himself will be seized in its full implications, and the liberty of the children of God will be made manifest.

The Christian, moreover, has lived in the close unity of the body of the Church, supported by the efforts of others, and himself giving impetus to the life of the whole. All the activities of the individual Christian have had their effects upon the whole body, and this interaction of individual upon individual and upon the Church will be revealed to the society of the faithful in all its social import. A collective illumination will aid the faithful to judge the universal moral order, and there will be no more room for the questioning of history; it will have yielded up its innermost secrets, and all the intertwining series of causes and effects will be laid bare. The labors of the saints will be seen in their full depth and extent, which exceed the dimension of their particular historical period. The collaboration of man with the labor of the eternal Father and Christ will be unmistakable. It will be the triumph of a society: The Church.

As the Christian has begun his life as a member of a society and has fostered that life within a society, so his final judgment will be social. The consummation of all things within the unity of the Mystical Body of Christ being now completed, the Christian will pass to the social life of the new Jerusalem.

—Robert W. Gleason: *At Evening We Shall Be Judged By Love*

Chapter 7
Rewards at the Judgment Seat

Every young Greek in the days of Paul had a special understanding of the *bema*. It was the seat of reward on which the umpire of the games sat, and from which he crowned the winners of events. What honor and dignity came from that place!

No wonder any price or sacrifice was thought to be worthwhile to be a winner in the Ithmian games (forerunner of the Olympic games). The "wreath of laurel" was worth every form of discipline and denial necessary to the athlete. Paul must have had the Ithmian games of the Greek peninsula in mind when he wrote in First Corinthians 9:25:

> And everyone who competes for the prize is temperate in all things. Now *they* do it to obtain a perishable crown, but we for an imperishable crown.

Contestants trained for years in grueling, difficult athletics. They brought themselves under complete control and abstained from anything which would put a damper on their effectiveness.

The Judgment Seat of Christ is similarly a place where rewards and losses are revealed. You've seen the contemporary examples: An Olympian will train four years for a brief moment of athletic test: a race, a jump, a demonstration, or a fight.

Worthy of the Prize!

I shall never forget one such event I witnessed on international television. Four young winners of Olympic gold for wrestling stood proudly on the stand, their ribbons and medals shining in the sun, as the band played their national anthem.

They had won! What dignity was theirs in this international parade of champions. No one noted the worth of the material composing their medals or ribbons, but everyone saw the worth of the men wearing such honors.

One of the winners reached with his hand to brush back a tear from his eye. They had won the victory! They were worthy of the prize!

Surely you see that image in its eternal application. When the Lord comes, Paul writes, "...each one's praise will come from God" (1 Corinthians 4:5). Discussing "that day" with the Corinthians, Paul writes, "If anyone's work which he has built on it endures, he will receive a reward" (1 Corinthians 3:14).

General William Booth, who also had a vision of the Judgment Seat of Christ, first commented on the indescribable music he heard:

> The whole firmament was filled as it were, with innumerable forms, each of beauty and dignity, far surpassing those with whom I had already made acquaintance. Here was a representative portion of the aristocracy of heaven accompanying the king...and now the procession was upon me. I had seen some of the pageants of earth — displays that required the power of mighty monarchs, and the wealth of great cities and nations to create — but they were each, or all combined, as the feeble light of a candle to a tropical sun in comparison with the tremendous scene which now spread itself before my astonished eyes.

And who made up this aristocracy of heaven? Booth answers:

> Nearest to the King were the patriarchs and apostles of ancient times. Next, rank after rank, came the holy martyrs who had died for Him. Then came the army of warriors who had fought for Him in every part of the world.

46

And around and abound, above and below, I beheld myriads and myriads of spirits who were never heard of on earth outside their own neighborhood, or beyond their own times who, with self-denying zeal and untiring toil had labored to extend God's Kingdom and to save the souls of men....

Rewards in the New Testament

The theme of rewards is a frequent New Testament concept:

- Great reward in heaven (Matthew 5:12)
- Rewarded openly for secret ministry (Matthew 6:4)
- A prophet's reward (Matthew 10:41)
- A righteous man's reward (Matthew 10:41)
- Reward according to works (Matthew 16:27)
- A due or honest reward (Luke 23:41)
- Reward reckoned not of works (Romans 4:4)
- The reward of our inheritance (Colossians 3:24)
- A reward matched to our labor (1 Timothy 5:18)
- A just reward (Hebrews 2:2)
- A full reward (2 John 8)

In addition, the scripture speaks of the potential of lost reward (Mark 9:41) and of being deceived out of our reward (Colossians 2:18).

Crowns As Rewards

Usually when the New Testament speaks of receiving a reward, it is in the form of a crown. These crowns are always the *stephanos*, or victor's crown, from an earlier Greek word meaning "to twine or wreathe." The victor's crown was the prize in the public games, and it was the symbol of honor and achievement.

Following the Lord's crown of thorns, a concordance will list these major New Testament crowns:

1. The incorruptible crown (1 Corinthians 9:25)

2. "My joy and crown" (Philippians 4:1), and "our hope, or joy, or crown of rejoicing" (1 Thessalonians 2:19).
3. The crown of righteousness (2 Timothy 4:8).
4. The crown of life (James 1:12).
5. The crown of glory (1 Peter 5:4).

Each of these crowns, as we shall briefly see, is a symbol of authority and usefulness in a Christian's life. They are awarded to Christians who have achieved a specific spiritual discipline. No wonder Paul writes:

> Therefore I run thus: not with uncertainty. Thus I fight: not as one who beats the air.
>
> But I discipline my body and bring it into subjection, lest, when I have preached to others, I myself should become disqualified.
>
> 1 Corinthians 9:26,27

And no wonder the Risen Christ warns the Church:

> "Behold, I come quickly! Hold fast what you have, that no one may take your crown."
>
> Revelation 3:11

Such discussion of crowns is meant to emphasize the honor, the award, and the presentation, not just to describe the crown or the reward.

Specific Crowns

We would be wrong, however, to view mention of crowns as merely speculative. Each crown is found in a passage dealing with such specific issues as:

- The believer's character and role
- The believer's fruitfulness and soul-winning
- The believer's hope and expectation
- The believer's endurance and acceptance of trial
- The believer's faithfulness and service, or ministry

Each of these crowns is worthy of a great deal of study and consideration. For our purpose here, however, let them simply serve as reminders, or "inventory checks," of the development of our Christian walk.

The Victor's Crown

1. The first crown we will study is the imperishable, or *victor's crown.*

We have previously viewed the text of First Corinthians 9:24-27, and we shall examine it further in the following chapter. It is one of the most revealing passages concerning the Apostle Paul's personal discipline. Let us first quote verses 24 through 27:

Do you not know that those who run in a race all run, but one receives the prize? Run in such a way that you may obtain it.

And everyone who competes for the prize is temperate in all things. Now they do it to obtain a perishable crown, but we for an imperishable crown.

Therefore I run thus: not for uncertainty. Thus I fight; not as one who beats the air.

But I discipline my body and bring it into subjection, lest, when I have preached to others, I myself should become disqualified.

Christian Awareness

Here Paul refers to the necessity of constant Christian awareness of both our real antagonist, Satan, and our specific goal, conforming to the likeness of Jesus.

We are not all alike. Every Christian begins his new life with a great variety of genetic, cultural, and environmental backgrounds.

Paul's answer to making the body subject and "slave" — to avoid falling in the race — will prove helpful in the life of every believer.

He doesn't suggest in the slightest the possibility that one might become castaway from his faith. Instead, he concentrates on the awful potential of failing to achieve our specific Christian purpose.

Think of the eternal victory ahead for the faithful runner when he stands before the Lord! This "crown" is the victory of fulfilling our Christian purpose.

Pressing Toward the Goal

In a similar way, the Apostle Paul is open and vulnerable in sharing with the Philippians:

> **Not that I have already attained, or am already perfect; but I press on, that I may lay hold of that for which Christ Jesus has also laid hold of me.**
>
> **Brethren, I do not count myself to have apprehended; but one thing I do, forgetting those things which are behind and reaching forward to those things which are ahead,**
>
> **I press toward the goal for the prize of the upward call of God in Christ Jesus.**
>
> **Philippians 3:12-14**

You and I, like ably trained athletes, must press toward the unchangeable personal direction of God for our lives. We cannot compare ourselves with others, and we must never look back (2 Corinthians 10:12; Luke 9:62). Anything obstructing our progress must be eliminated.

The norm for our lives must be denial for Christ's sake and for the calling of God upon our lives.

In two Bible passages, we are taught to get rid of flowing garments which would impede the speed and progress of our race. Peter said, "Gird up the loins of your mind" (1 Peter 1:13).

Likewise, the writer to the Hebrews said:

> **...let us lay aside every weight, and the sin which so easily ensnares us, and let us run with endurance the race that is set before us, looking unto Jesus, the author and finisher of our faith**
>
> **Hebrews 12:1,2**

The contestant in a race eliminated unnecessary clothing. The race is real, and the imperishable crown awaits the victorious racer at the hands of our lovely Lord.

The Soul-Winner's Crown

2. The New Testament clearly concentrates on the fruitfulness, or soul-winning activities of the believer's life.

Referring to those he had won to Christ, the Apostle Paul wrote:

> **For what is our hope, or joy, or crown of rejoicing? Is it not even *you* in the presence of our Lord Jesus Christ at His coming?**
>
> **For you are our glory and joy.**
>
> 1 Thessalonians 2:19,20

Paul says he will recognize those he had won to Christ, and he will joy in them in the presence of the Lord.

The principal business of the Christian is to share the faith of Jesus Christ with others!

> **The fruit of the righteous is a tree of life, And he who wins souls is wise.**
>
> Proverbs 11:30

The closing words of the Epistle of James are powerful:

> **...let him know that he who turns a sinner from the error of his way will save a soul from death and cover a multitude of sins.**
>
> James 5:20

The human spirit or soul has inestimable value in the sight of God. The very coming of Jesus Christ to earth is expressed as a gift from God so that men might not perish, "...but have everlasting life" (John 3:16). When one sinner repents, our Lord reveals, "...there is joy in the presence of the angels of God..." (Luke 15:10).

Lost Opportunities

The agony of General Booth's vision of the Judgment Seat of Christ had to do mostly with lost opportunities concerning Christian witness. He writes:

> Nevertheless, a further glance at my record appalled me, for there was written therein — leaving out, as I have said, the sins of commission — there was written the exact daily record of the whole of my past life! In fact it went much deeper, because it described in full detail the object for which I had lived. It recorded my thoughts and feelings and actions — how and for what I had employed my time, my money, my influence, and all the other talents and gifts which God had intrusted me with to spend for His glory and for the salvation of the lost.... I was reminded how, instead of fighting His battles, instead of saving souls by bringing them to His feet, and so preparing them for admission into this lovely place, I had been on the contrary, intent on earthly things, selfishly seeking my own, spending my life in practical unbelief, disloyalty and disobedience.

How many souls have we won for Christ? Have we faithfully sown seed, travailed in prayer, and bought up our opportunities for harvest?

Soul-winning comes through the Word of God used by the Holy Spirit to convict and convince. What a reward for those who, by loving God's Word, are earnest in their personal work for Christ. As Paul told the Philippians:

> **...my beloved and longed-for brethren, my joy and crown, so stand fast in the Lord, beloved.**
>
> **Philippians 4:1**

The Crown of Righteousness

3. The third crown named in the New Testament order of the chronology of reward is a crown of righteousness.

This crown is specifically dealt with in Second Timothy 4:5-8. Some believe these are the last words Paul wrote. They were directed tenderly at his beloved Timothy as he himself gazed steadfastly at martyrdom. Paul's words are challenging and prophetic. In firm, but personal language, he writes:

> **But you be watchful in all things, endure afflictions, do the work of an evangelist, fulfill your ministry.**
>
> **For I am already being poured out as a drink offering, and the time of my departure is at hand.**
>
> **I have fought the good fight, I have finished the race, I have kept the faith.**
>
> **Finally, there is laid up for me the crown of righteousness, which the Lord, the righteous Judge, will give me on that Day, and not to me only, but also to all who have loved His appearing.**
>
> **2 Timothy 4:5-8**

Paul's coming appearance before the judgment seat of Rome held no fear for the apostle. His eye was watchfully upon the *bema* of the Lord instead. Paul suggests here a special crown of righteousness for watchers and lovers of the Lord's appearing.

I personally believe that these words address the issue of motive. What is commended and what will be rewarded is an eye "single" to the glory of the Lord. Christ's appearing, the hope of the believer, also motivates the believer to a life of purity (1 John 3:3). We are to live and act always mindful that "the Lord is at hand" (Philippians 4:5).

The Crown of Life

4. Fourth on the *bema* table of rewards is what the Apostle James calls "the crown of life." This reward is shown by context, however, to concern the believer's endurance and acceptance of trial.

It is a reward of unusual significance to believers today. On the one hand, there is unheralded and incomparable suffering in much of the Christian Church; and on the other hand, many Christians deny that suffering is to be experienced by believers.

My brethren, count it all joy when you fall into various trials,

knowing that the testing of your faith produces patience...

Blessed is the man who endures temptation; for when he has been proved, he will receive the crown of life which the Lord has promised to those who love Him.

James 1:2,3,12

The word "temptation" is startling and revealing. It comes from a verb meaning "to test" or "scrutinize," which is an entirely different word from that used in James 1:13,14. There the word means "temptation to sin." Here it is a putting to the proof, or an examination. It is the same as an assay of metal, which proves its quality and caliber.

"In the world," Jesus promised, "you will have tribulation; but be of good cheer, I have overcome the world" (John 16:33). As is customary in the New Testament, the word translated "tribulation" is *thlipsis* in the original Greek. *Thlipsis* is far more accurately translated — *pressure!*

The Arena of Proving

How can even a casual reading of the first chapter of James fail to reveal that "enduring" testing and "loving Him" are integrally connected? New Testament Christians often were forced to prove their faith literally by facing wild animals in the arena. The believer today is scheduled for the arena of proving in his Christian life, too.

It was said of Joseph in the Old Testament, "Until the time that His word came to pass, the word of the Lord *tested* him" (Psalm 105:19).

The believer may pout and demand an end to his trial and, like spoiled children quoting proof texts from scripture, may be released from his trial. James, however, says in essence, "Happy is the man who can withstand the test." No one is excepted from God's proving."

Hupomone, the word translated "endure," is the strongest possible word for courageous and triumphant fortitude and strength. It is not a passive position. One translator suggests that James pleads for a spirit which can bear things not with resignation, "but with blazing hope."

The Aristocracy of Heaven

Such a Christian is *dokimos* — approved after testing, the exact opposite of the fearful *adokimos* of Paul's fear in First Corinthians 9 — someone who is disqualified or cast away.

To the victor is the honor of a living crown, a crown of life. A casual reading of *Fox's Book of Martyrs* or any of a host of Christian biographies throughout Church history will prepare you for this special group at the *bema* seat. General Booth described them as "the aristocracy of heaven accompanying the King."

Later, Booth describes the way Jesus looked at him: "It was not pain, and yet it was not pleasure," he writes. "It was not anger and yet it was not approval."

Here is another quotation from his vision:

> That face, that divine face, seemed to say to me, for language was not needed to convey to the very depths of my soul what His feelings were to me: "Thou wilt feel thyself little in harmony with these, once the companions of My tribulations and now of My glory, who counted not their lives dear unto themselves in order that they might bring honor to me and salvation to men." And he gave a look of admiration at the host of apostles and martyrs and warriors gathered around Him.
>
> How visible indeed will be that moment of special honor and dignity, when it will be proclaimed, "Please step forward, all those to receive the crown of life, promised by our beloved Lord to those having endured trial and continued to love the Lord."

The Shepherd's Crown

5. The fifth and final crown we will examine in this discussion is a unique award for those who faithfully served in

the most Christlike calling of ministry: shepherding, or caring for the Church.

It is Peter who caught this special glimpse of the Judgment Seat of Christ:

> **The elders who are among you I exhort, I who am a fellow elder and a witness of the sufferings of Christ, and also a partaker of the glory that will be revealed:**
>
> **Shepherd the flock of God which is among you, serving as overseers, not by constraint but willingly, not for dishonest gain but eagerly;**
>
> **nor as being lords over those entrusted to you, but being examples to the flock;**
>
> **and when the Chief Shepherd appears, you will receive the crown of glory that does not fade away.**

> **1 Peter 5:1-4**

Conditions of Leadership

This doubtless underscores both the value Christ places in His Church and the responsibility of those who are appointed as leaders and under-shepherds within it. Specific conditions of leadership are spelled out in this passage.

Leaders, for example, are not to domineer or seek for personal gain. Above all, their service is to be done "eagerly" — one of the strongest expressions in the Greek language to describe "zealously, with enthusiasm, and devoted zeal."

Ministry can be clouded, as Balaam's was,[1] by the promise of earthly or commercial reward. Others may serve by compulsion and the pressure of others. There is, however, available to all the Spirit of the Great Shepherd to leave all for the caring and nurturing of the sheep.

Personally, I do not believe that this "unfading crown" is directed only to those in so-called full-time ministry. More and more the day reveals the need for nurture, care, feeding, and tending, especially of the young and the new convert. Surely Jesus' words in John 21 have a broader application than the obvious restoration of Peter.

"Do you love Me?" Jesus asked Peter.

"Oh, yes, beloved Lord. More than these. More than anything."

"Then feed my lambs. Tend my sheep. Feed my sheep," the Lord replies.

Certainly the spotlights of eternity will beam especially bright as these faithful folk step forward to the dias:

"Those receiving the crown of glory — the Lord's special honor and dignity for sharing His own shepherding heart and ministry — please step forward."

"It will be worth it all," wrote the dear, suffering Esther Kerr Rusthoi, "when we see Jesus. Life's trials will seem so small when we see Him. One glimpse of His dear face, all sorrows will erase. So bravely run the race, 'til we see Christ."

---

[1]Balaam appears commonly in the Old and New Testaments as an examlpe of an evil artist, a prophet who would sell his skill for the proper price, without reference to the Word of God (Numbers 22-24)

*B*ut the great crowd of sinners not hostile to God will rise again not to glory but to be submitted to scrutiny. The man who is to reveal and render an account of his actions, and be approved or condemned according to his differing deeds, cannot sit with the saint.

Those who are ignorant of the law will fall, scattered in the disorder; he who fell while living under the law will be judged by the law. Fire will be the judge, and will rush through every deed. Every act that the flame does not consume but approves will be allotted eternal reward. He who has done deeds which must be burned will suffer injury, but will safely escape the flames; yet wretched because of the marks on his charred body, he will preserve his life without glory. He was conquered by the flesh, but not perverted in mind; therefore, in spite of his denying to the law the allegiance which was its due, by his frequent involvement in many sins, he will never be exiled from the shores of salvation, for he preserves the eternal glory of the faith.

So as long as all of us in this world maintain life's course and our days continue, we must keep our feet firmly on the right path, and not be seduced onto the slippery and broad highway. It is better to struggle on the narrow path and to enter by strenuous exertion. God gladly acknowledges the way of good men, but the path of the godless will be destroyed and leveled.

—Paulinus of Nola: *As The Wind Whirls*

Chapter 8
The Need for Action

The Apostle Paul was not given to frequent personal discussion. He could, however, be very vulnerable at times about his life and ministry.

In First Corinthians 9, we find one such transparent defense of his apostolic office and its unclaimed privileges and rights. It is a typical mixed list of freedoms through Christ, but restrictions by choice. I suggest to you that the passage is particularly applicable to our study on the Judgment Seat of Christ:

> Do you not know that those who run in a race all run, but one receives the prize? Run in such a way that you may obtain it.
>
> And everyone who competes for the prize is temperate in all things. Now they do it to obtain a perishable crown, but we for an imperishable crown.
>
> Therefore I run thus: not with uncertainty. Thus I fight: not as one who beats the air.
>
> But I discipline my body and bring it into subjection, lest, when I have preached to others, I myself should become disqualified.
>
> 1 Corinthians 9:24-27

Scholars often call attention to this passage because of the strong athletic language used. The Isthmian games of Greece were a familiar image to everyone in the first century. Winners received not only the laurel crown from the *bema* seat, but through that recognition they achieved fame, wealth, and popularity not unlike our modern Olympian gold medal winners.

Our Challenge

Paul says that the believer does not run as one without fixed and certain goals. He is not shadow-boxing, or failing to make his strikes tell. The believer is aware of the intense challenge of his experience.

This is definitely not a passage speaking of some agonizing uncertainty in attempting to win eternal life. It is the pattern of responsible discipline in the fulfillment of Christian purpose and ministry.

The Greek word for race is *agon* (or "agony"). The Christian life is not a bed of roses. Christian victory and warfare are not for cream puffs. This is war! And the enemy we fight is not, first of all, the devil. Instead, it is our flesh — the predisposition within our unredeemed body, within our human nature, to demand ease and avoid discipline.

The horrendous potential is that by yielding to our flesh we are "disqualified," or *adokimos*, rejected as unusable, benched by the coach at the most strategic moment of the contest!

To avoid this, the apostle uses two verbs concerning his action upon his own body which imply the utmost in rigorous, almost sadistic control, in order that the body might serve and not hinder his progress toward the goal of Christian victory and ultimate reward.

"I discipline my body," one translation reads. Actually, it is a strong word for "striking under the eye, or beating black and blue." One could paraphrase it, "I turn the boxing glove upon my own body, and I beat my flesh black and blue." Paul says that his body must never become the enemy to his spiritual purpose; therefore, he buffets it!

Again, the apostle says that he works on the body to "bring it into subjection." Here, too, the strength of the original language is almost untranslatable. It means to lead into slavery, or to make or treat as a slave. Oh, reader, you must understand this intensity!

Standing before our Lord Jesus Christ at His *bema*, I shall receive "the things done in the body, according to what...I have done, whether good or bad" (2 Corinthians 5:10) — because the *bema* is not like the reward stand of a modern Olympiad.

That understanding requires very specific discipline and choice during these days of my experience in the body. No wonder, in a parallel passage concerning the Christian race and discipline, the Word admonishes:

> **Therefore, since we are receiving a kingdom which cannot be shaken, let us have grace, by which we may serve God acceptably with reverence and godly fear.**
>
> **For our God is a consuming fire.**
>
> **Hebrews 12:28,29**

The Double Loss

When a believer fails to live within God's will and purpose, there is a tragic double loss. The first, the earthly life, is joyless, powerless, and without intimate fellowship with God. Second, at the Judgment Seat of Christ, confronted with God's real purpose and intention for his life, that believer suffers the loss of all things.

He sees the plan of God for his life — had God had His way — and he must compare it eternally with the pittance of his own poor human response!

But there is a further word for us at this time. The early race of the believer is more accurately a "trial run," or an elimination heat. What must be understood is that the real stake is not only recognition or reward, but position and responsibility for eternity.

Your Actions Determine Your Role

Like athletes working to make the team, the believer's discipline, or lack of it, plays a role in determining his eternal position. Nothing is clearer and more frightening: *What I do in eternity is being determined by my choices here!*

God's grace manifested in so great a salvation gets the believer into heaven, but it is the believer's earth-choices and works which determine what he will do and be once he gets there!

Dr. C. S. Lovett, author and president of Personal Christianity, wrote in a recent article:

Most people think of the Lord's coming as ushering in an eternal vacation. But it just isn't so. God is a busy Person, and industrious Creator. His most faithful servants will of necessity be the closest to Him. This is why the top places of heaven must go to those who sacrifice their interests to put Christ ahead of everything else — family included. There will be different ranks in heaven. The order will descend from top positions clear to ghettos. There'll be poor Christians there. God can't be blamed when men throw away the one opportunity of this life. Every Christian can be as rich as he wants, but it means putting Jesus ahead of everything else."

These are strong and convicting words. Jesus' longest and most-developed parable concerned house-stewards, or servants left in charge of money, land, or people in the absence of their master.

Faithfulness Examined

Upon the master's return, these servants were examined concerning their faithfulness. The results were increased assignments, such as being put in charge of cities or enlarged sums of money for continuing, faithful investment.

The unfaithful, however, faced frightful loss and judgment.

You may wish further study of these parables in Matthew 25:14-46, Matthew 24:45-51, Luke 12:35-46, Luke 16:1-13, and Luke 17:5-10. This list is certainly not exhaustive, but it will quickly give the reader a feeling for this greatest of all perspectives and parables of Christian responsibility.

The believer's life on this earth is his only arena for change and fruitfulness. After all, the nature of eternity is changeless. Therefore, the time to become like Jesus, being conformed to His likeness, is during this earthly Christian experience of trial and faith.

If Jesus came for the Church today, I must enter heaven *as I am at this moment!* The time for maturing and change is *now* in the period of the Lord's training [of His people?].

"We stop maturing when Jesus comes," Dr. Lovett writes. "Our desire to serve Him and be like Him will be SET. From then on it will neither increase nor decrease. In other words, you and I will never be any closer to Christ, *throughout eternity,* than we are when He comes. That's the point of the judgment."

Punishments and Rewards

Don't be deceived. There are degrees and levels of punishment and reward. Jesus made comparisons of judgment by frequently using the expressions "more tolerable" (Matthew 10:15; 11:21-24) and "greater damnation" (Matthew 23:14), as well as "many stripes" or "few" (Luke 12:48).

This is supported in the later New Testament theological development of Romans 2. In the same way, as we are consistently seeing, the Judgment Seat of Christ will reveal everything from great faithfulness and reward to empty-handed believers who only "suffer loss."

The apocalyptic pictures of heaven all show differences in proximity to the Throne of God. The reward for service is more assignments to do. The very closing pictures in the Bible of the glories of eternity include the absence of curse and night. The glories of God's river and throne are there, "...and His servants shall serve Him. They shall see His face, and His name shall be on their foreheads" (Revelation 22:3,4).

"Weeping and Wailing" on That Day

My friend who stood before a circle of blackened earth is a symbol of many believers who are saved by grace, but through lack of obedience and sacrificial service will "weep and wail" (Matthew 25:34).

"But all Christians will be perfect then," you say.

Yes, just like all light bulbs or car engines may be perfect, but not all have the same wattage or power.

The Christian's love is measured by obedience. The Christian's life is a series of choices toward discipline, change, fruitfulness, and the likeness of the Son Himself.
Christians are not ready until they have made themselves ready (Revelation 19:7).

Christians will stand before Jesus Christ, the heavenly Bridegroom, clad not only in the basic tunic or undergarment provided for everyone by the righteousness of Jesus Christ, but "arrayed in fine linen, clean and bright, for the fine linen is the righteous acts of the saints" (Revelation 19:8).

Can there be any doubt that while some of those garments will be dazzling and beautiful, other Christians will stand ashamed, clad only in basic white?

God's Dream for Our Life

The greatest horror of the Judgment Seat of Christ will not be the loss of our works, but the revelation of His purpose. When we truly see what God's gracious dream for our life included — when we know what His earnest expectations were for us — that will be the moment of our greatest loss. Oh, to catch that intent; to understand God's dream for us!

I discipline my body and bring it into subjection, lest, when I have preached to others..." — I am benched!

The judgment seat of Christ is the TERROR of Christianity. Christians who use their time, money, and talents for self-living, instead of Christ, should tremble at the thought. What makes it so frightening? Our future relationship to Jesus is based on it, in that day, our earthly record will be evaluated to determine our eternal status, in heaven. The decision rendered there is permanent! See now why I urge believers to get ready for Jesus' coming? Faithfulness to Christ as Lord is going to be the basis of that judgment. What we have done to make Christ Lord is all that will count.

—C. S. Lovett

Chapter 9
Taking the Exam

The day I walked into that college classroom, having skipped two weeks of classes, is a vivid example of what many believers will feel when they face Christ's judgment seat.

After my best friend informed me of the exam, knowing I was totally unprepared, I had rushed out to the staircase, hoping to intercept the professor before he came into the classroom.

Sure enough, I heard Dr. Rogers coming up the stairs whistling in his inimitable off-key manner. He looked up at me over the top of his glasses and said, "Good morning, Mr. Howard."

"Dr. Rogers, sir..." I stuttered. "Sir, I understand you're giving a mid-semester exam this morning...."

"That's correct," he said, frowning, probably knowing what was coming next.

"Sir, my head is as empty as my notebook! I don't even know what chapters you've been studying. May I *please* prepare and take the exam tomorrow?"

What I told him was more than true: I had missed five lectures and five daily assignments. I didn't have the slightest idea of what was expected of me on the midterm examination!

That normally kind and truly Christian instructor looked at me and said firmly, "Mr. Howard, I don't approve of this attendance policy. I can't punish you for missing classes, but you *must* take the exam this morning with your fellow students or receive an automatic failure in this class!"

Unprepared for the Judgment Seat

Isn't that the quandary that many of us now face? There's an established test-date, but it's unexpected and unplanned for by many believers. What subjects will be covered in the examination? How can a Christian prepare for it? What material has been assigned?

Perhaps it's time for a check list. In addition to generalities, such as "words" and "life," do we have any biblical understanding of what is being dealt with at the Judgment Seat of Christ? If so, what is it, and how should we respond?

A quick look at the issues which the Apostle Paul addresses in First Corinthians 3 and 4 — his longest developed teaching on the Judgment Seat of Christ — is revealing.

Here Paul discusses the Christian's failure to grow and the carnality that results; spiritual divisiveness and its terrible harvest; the necessity of productivity or fruitfulness; the issue of conformity as "God's own building"; the matter of holy maintenance of the temple of God, free from defilement; the motive of life as God's glory; and faithfulness in our life's assignment as a servant and a steward.

If we were to take the above issues as a check list, we could examine other biblical examples whenever the subjects of: *growth, fellowship, fruitfulness, conformity to God's will, holiness, purity of purpose and motive,* and *faithfulness* are the focus. Even a simple examination of such a check list would demand a book in itself!

The Believer's Responsibilities

Another, perhaps simpler, way of arranging scriptural understanding on the subject is to see that the believer is responsible and will be judged on three basic areas of conduct:

1. How he has affected *himself* and his destiny under God by his choices, activities, and motives.

2. How he has affected *others* by the conduct of his life.
3. How he has affected *God* and the Kingdom of God in the "living out" of his Christian experience.

These three categories are meant to allow us to carefully examine some details of biblical instruction. These are simply helps, not divinely inspired divisions.

A. God Cares About Me

How often I have heard believers say something like, "Well, I'm not hurting anyone else by this activity. After all, it's my life."

The world frequently states this in its popular philosophy through music and the media in general. "It's *my* life" or, "I did it *my* way," they say.

We see in scripture that the believer is a person of infinite value to God. The concept of Redemption always implies that a purchase or price is paid, not only for the person's freedom, for toward his or her future usefulness.

Saved to Serve

We are redeemed to be used, and God's plans for us are good. He lovingly wills and supplies toward our very best. Therefore, the Judgment Seat of Christ will reveal and evaluate our words, conversations, and doctrine.

A quick look through Matthew 12:32-37, Romans 14:5, and even Romans 2:14-16, will show how important it is to know, to be "fully persuaded," and to speak the truth fully.

Romans 14 especially makes the issue of confidence and faith the ultimate umpire or choice for one's personal conviction. I must walk out all my life by faith, for whatever does not come from faith is sin.

I am a dream of God! The issue of my life and its fulfillment has high priority on the scales of God's justice at the Judgment Seat of Christ.

Some have felt that self-depreciation is somehow a mark of true holiness. Nothing is further from what the Bible states.

Accepting and acting fully and uncompromisingly according to my gifts and differences should be my spiritual goal.

It is only necessary that I glorify God, for whatever differences I possess are a gift from the Father (1 Corinthians 4:7).

God's Plan for You Is Good

There is a plan of God for every life. It will always represent not only the glory of God, but the full joy and true fulfillment of each person's personal life. I believe God was not addressing the following words only to the nation of Judah when He said:

"For I know the thoughts that I think toward you," says the Lord, "thoughts of peace and not of evil, to give you a future and a hope."

Jeremiah 29:11

Therefore, what I do which affects myself is highly significant. This includes habits, thought patterns, negative associations or self-depreciation, choices, and confession.

"Do you have faith?" Paul asks. "Have it to yourself before God. Happy is he who does not condemn himself in what he approves" (Romans 14:22).

B. My Life Affects Others

No person lives completely unto himself. People are affected around us every day by the living-out of our Christian experience.

It is no wonder, therefore, that such is an issue at the Judgment Seat of Christ. Paul clearly marks the relationship of these issues in Romans 14, when he asks:

But why do you judge your brother? Or why do you show contempt for your brother? For we shall all stand before the judgment seat of Christ.

For it is written, "As I live, says the Lord, Every knee shall bow to Me, and every tongue shall confess to God."

So then each of us shall give account of himself to God.

Therefore let us not judge one another anymore, but rather resolve this, not to put a stumbling block or a cause to fall in our brother's way.

Romans 14:11-13

Offending the Brethren

We can offend others by broken promises, wrong and unfair dealings, idle words and foolishness, dishonesty and lack of integrity, slander and quarreling. Ephesians 4 and 5, Colossians 3, and Galatians 5 are, with Romans 12 and 14, key passages on this issue of relationships with others.

Even in pure cases of personal knowledge and faith, the believer acts to the priority on how they will affect a brother's needs (1 Corinthians 8:11-13).

Even when there is a clear right or privilege involved, the believer yields for a brother's needs, "...lest we hinder the gospel of Christ" (1 Corinthians 9:12).

These scriptures are in no way to bring the individual believer to a place of life-paralysis, affected by the judgment and conviction of every other negative believer.

"But with me it is a very small thing that I should be judged by you or by a human court," Paul writes. "In fact, I do not even judge myself...but He who judges me is the Lord" (1 Corinthians 4:3,4).

What they do, however, is to leave a clear area of self-examination, knowing that will be an issue of scrutiny at the Judgment Seat of Christ.

How telling are these words to the Ephesians:

> **For you were once darkness, but now you are light in the Lord. Walk as children of light....**
>
> **Ephesians 5:8**

C. My Life Is Important to God

The integral relationship of the individual to the purposes and Kingdom of God is one of scriptures's most frequently addressed issues.

The believer is a member of Christ's Body, and his personal choices should imitate Jesus Christ (1 Corinthians 6:15-17).

The world, in associating with the believer, considers that it has come to Christ Himself (Mark 9:14-17). The belief or lack of belief in Jesus Christ by the world at large is deeply affected by the believer's actions (John 7:21,23).

The Value of the Individual

Paul declares, "...you are God's field, you are God's building" (1 Corinthians 3:9). J. B. Phillips has beautifully paraphrased that verse as: "You are a field under God's cultivation, you are a building being built to God's specifications." In both these illustrations, there is an imminent investment and value by God in the individual believer.

Jesus frequently spoke of the owner looking for increase and fruitfulness in a field, or the expectation from a tree's productivity.

My life, in other words, has a direct bearing on the Kingdom of God. I would rather be thrown naked into a pit of rattlesnakes than to cause division and disunity within the Body for which Christ died.

First Corinthians 3 and 4, Romans 12, and Ephesians 4 and 5 speak of the things which the believer does which affect God and His purpose.

No more convicting command exists in the Holy Scripture than this:

And do not grieve the Holy Spirit of God, by whom you were sealed for the day of redemption.

Ephesians 4:30

The fourth and fifth chapters of Ephesians offer admonition and teaching, challenging the believer to:

1. Walk in unity (4:1-16)

2. Walk in holiness (4:17-32)

3. Walk in love (5:1-7)

4. Walk in light (5:8-14)

5. Walk in wisdom and order (5:15-6:9)

Indeed, a significant portion of Christ's *bema* judgment for us will pertain to the effect we have had upon the Kingdom of God.

The Vision That Changed Booth's Life

When the great General William Booth, ultimate founder of the Salvation Army, had the phenomenal vision of the Judgment Seat of Christ, he was already zealously serving God.

However, the warning of the vision both intensified his future service and, as he shared, became a life-changing admonition to thousands of others.

In the vision, Booth, at the brink of death, enters heaven and is confronted by countless believers asking him for specific reports of loved ones still on earth — loved ones he'd had opportunities to witness to concerning Jesus Christ!

At one point, he cries out, "Oh my God, is this heaven? Will these questionings go on forever? Will the meanness and selfishness of my past life haunt me throughout eternity? What shall I do? Can I not go back to earth, and do something to redeem myself from this wretched sense of unworthiness? Can I not live my life over again?"

The First Day of the Rest of My Life

My reaction was the same that spring evening when I awoke in terror, sweaty and crying, after my vision of the Judgment Seat of Christ. I felt washed and cleansed, determined and excited.

It was indeed "the first day of the rest of my life!" I could never be the same! Every day would now, at some point, bear record to its truest destiny.

From this moment on, I took the responsibility to be accountable for all of my actions, knowing they would count for eternity. Life could never be the same for me again.

Is This Your Life?

By General William Booth

I had a very strange vision the other day. And I have been greatly perplexed as to whether or not I should tell it to others. The chief difficulty I find concerning it is that it seems to lay me open to the charge of being too severe, in seeming to shut out of heaven a great multitude who are expecting to go there. Because I portray the gate narrower than the Bible is supposed to make it.

In this it will be considered, perhaps, that the vision I received is at fault, and therefore, somewhat misleads. But on its behalf I may suggest that as heaven is, as the negro said, "a mighty big place," it may be only some special part of the vast Continent of Blessedness that is referred to.

In my vision I thought that so far as the world was concerned, Agur's prayer was answered in regard to me, for I had neither poverty nor riches. All my wants were supplied. I had leisure, and friends, and home, and all that was necessary to make me happy.

Then also, I thought that I was a Christian. Most of my close friends professed to be the same. We visited together at each other's homes, joined in amusements, business, politics and many other things. In short, we bought and sold, and married, and acted as though the world we were in were going to last forever.

In this vision I was one who was active in religious activities. In fact, I considered myself to be quite a shining light. I always attended church on Sunday and I taught in the Sunday School. Now and then, though not very often, I visited the sick. And in addition to these good deeds I gave a little money to support Christian work.

In all this I was quite sincere. I had no idea of playing the hypocrite. It's true that I didn't stop to consider what Christianity really was, although I talked freely enough about it at times, and pitied people who didn't profess to be Christians.

I seldom, if ever, considered what Jesus Christ required. Nor was I very concerned about the lost, although I heard these matters occasionally discussed in my presence. I had gotten into a definite rut in thought and action and profession. And I went on from day to day, hoping that everything would turn out all right in the end.

But in my vision I thought that without any apparent warning a dangerous fever seized me. I became terribly sick all of a sudden. In fact, in just a few hours I was brought to the very brink of death. This was serious business, indeed. Everyone about me was in great confusion. And those who loved me were paralyzed with fear.

Some took action. The proper medicines were administered. There were consultations among several physicians. And the members of my family hurried to my side from far and near. Friends and acquaintances came.

I was given the best medical care possible — but all proved in vain.

I could feel that the medicines weren't helping. And yet I didn't feel anything very much. I don't know whether this was because of the suddenness of the sickness or the deadening character of the narcotics which the physicians gave me. But strangely enough I seemed to be the least disturbed person in the place.

I felt as though I were in a dream. I knew I was ill — dangerously ill — because a relative had insisted on my being informed of my real condition. And yet I was not disturbed about the fact. I thought I would recover. Most people do, I suppose, until the hand of death is actually upon them.

And if I did not recover, I had no reason to be terribly concerned, because, wasn't I a Christian? Hadn't I been converted? Didn't I believe the Bible? Why should I fear?

And wasn't I continually hearing hymns being sung and prayers offered that I might be restored to health, and if not, that I might pass away without suffering, and have a good time of it in heaven?

But even so, disquieting thoughts did cross my mind — because I couldn't keep out questions that kept arising as to whether I had truly followed Jesus Christ and had done my duty to a perishing world with my time and influence, and money and family. And questions would come and go that were very difficult indeed to answer. Yet it was all in a dreamy way. How could it be otherwise, with the burning fever lapping up the vital current, and my brain all benumbed, and my energies laid prostrate.

So when I complained that I didn't have much joy or assurance, I quite naturally agreed readily to the suggestion that my condition prevented this. And I felt, moreover, that if I were not "ready" I had neither the time nor energy to begin so serious a business over again as the salvation of my soul. Besides, how could I confess that I had been mistaken all these years, and that my life had been a failure? No! It was too late, and I was too ill for any such confession.

One thing I could do, and that I did. I cast myself, with what force of soul I had left, on the mercy of my Savior. And again and again I repeated a verse which had always been a favorite of mine:

"I am a poor sinner, just nothing at all,
But Jesus Christ is my all in all."

It was with this sentence on my lips — a sentence taken up and reproduced at my funeral service — that a cold numbness seemed to come creeping over me, and a great difficulty of breathing seized me. My friends were alarmed. I read it in their faces. Some prayed, while others wept. And my dear ones moistened my lips and kissed my brow.

Meanwhile a strange faintness seized me. I lost consciousness. My next sensation was altogether beyond description. It was the thrill of a new and celestial existence. I was in heaven.

After the first feeling of surprise had somewhat subsided, I looked around me, and took in the situation. It was way beyond anything of earth — positively delightful. And yet some of the more beautiful scenes and sounds and feelings of the world I had just left appeared to be repeated in my new experience in enchanting fashion. Still no human eyes ever beheld such perfection, such beauty. No earthly ear ever heard such music. No human heart ever experienced such ecstasy, as it was my privilege to see, hear, and feel in the celestial country.

Above me was the loveliest of blue skies. Around me was an atmosphere so balmy that it made my whole physical frame vibrate with pleasure. Flowing by the bank of roses on which I found myself reclining was the clearest and purest water of a river that seemed to dance with delight to its own murmurings. The trees that grew upon the banks were covered with the greenest foliage, and laden with most delicious fruit — sweet beyond all earthly sweetness. And by lifting up my hand I could pluck and taste.

In every direction above and around me the whole air seemed not only to be laden with the sweetest perfumes coming from the fairest flowers, but filled with the fairest forms. For, floating around me were beautiful beings whom I felt by instinct were angels and archangels, seraph and seraphim, cherub and cherubim, together with the perfect blood-washed saints who had come from our own world. They were sometimes far, and again coming nearer.

The whole sky at times seemed to be full of white-winged, happy, worshiping, joyous beings. And the whole country, apparently of limitless extent, was filled with a blissful ecstasy that could only be known by being experienced.

You may perhaps imagine my sensation. At first I was swallowed up with a sort of ecstatic intoxication, which feeling was immediately enhanced by the consciousness that I was safe, saved, to suffer and sin no more.

And then suddenly, a new set of feelings began to creep over me. Strange as it may seem, I felt somewhat lonely and a little sad, even in the midst of this infinite state of bliss. Because up to this moment I was alone. Not one of the bright beings who were soaring and singing in the bright ether above me, nor the ones who were hastening hither and thither, as though bent upon some high mission, had spoken to me or approached me.

I was alone in heaven! Then, in a still stranger and mysterious way, I appeared to feel in myself a sort of unfitness for the society of those pure beings who were sailing around me in indescribable loveliness. How could it be? Had I come there by mistake? Was I not counted worthy of this glorious inheritance? It was indeed a mystery.

My thoughts went back to earth. And all before me, as though unfolded by an angel's hand, the record of my past life was unrolled before my eyes. What a record it was! I glanced over it. And in a glance I seemed to master its entire contents — so rapidly, indeed, that I became conscious of a marvelous quickening of my intellectual powers. I realized that I could take in and understand in a moment what would have required a day with my poor, darkened faculties on earth.

With my quickened mind, I saw, to my delight, at that very first glance, that this register of my earthly existence — the Divine biography of my life — contained no record of any misdeeds before my conversion. Indeed, that part of my life seemed to be very much of a blank. I further perceived that neither was there any record of the sins I had done since that time. It was as though some friendly hand had gone through the roll and blotted out the record of the evil doings of my life. This was very gratifying. I felt like shouting praises to God, who had delivered me from the pain of having these things staring me in the face in this beautiful, holy land, among all these holy beings, where it seemed to me that the very memory of sin would defile.

Nevertheless, a further glance at my record appalled me, for there was written therein — leaving out, as I have said, the sins of commission — there was written the exact daily record of the whole of my past life! In fact, it went much deeper, because it described in full detail the object for which I had lived. It recorded my thoughts and feelings and actions — how and for what I had employed my time, my money, my influence, and all the other talents and gifts which God had intrusted me with to spend for His glory and for the salvation of the lost.

Every chapter of this record carried my thoughts back to the condition of the world I had left. And there came up before my eyes a vivid picture of its hatred for God, its rejection of Christ, its wickedness, with all the wretchedness and destitution and abomination. It utterly appalled me. Also into my ears there came a hurricane of cursing and blasphemy, and a wail of anguish and woe that stunned me.

I had seen these sights and had heard these sounds before, not too often, it is true, because I had hid myself from them. But now they blinded and stunned me. They appeared a million times blacker and more vile, more wretched and piteous, than they had ever seemed before!

I felt like putting my hands before my eyes, and my fingers in my ears to shut these things out from sight and hearing, so intensely real and present did they seem. They wrung my soul with sorrow and self-reproach, because on the "Record of Memory" I saw how I had occupied myself during the few years which I had been allowed to live amidst all these miseries, after Jesus Christ had called me to be His soldier. I was reminded how, instead of fighting His battles, instead of saving souls by bringing them to His feet, and so preparing them for admission into this lovely place, I had been on the contrary, intent on earthly things, selfishly seeking my own, spending my life in practical unbelief, disloyalty and disobedience.

I felt sick at heart. Oh, if at that moment I could have crept out of the "land of pure delight" about which I had sung so much in the past, and could have gone back to the world of darkness, sin and misery, which I had just left — if I could but spend another lifetime among the lost and dying, and truly follow my Lord!

But that could not be. My opportunities of earth were past. Heaven must now be my dwelling forever. And contradictory as it may seem, this thought filled my soul with unspeakable regret.

And then came another thought, more wild than any that had gone before it. (You must remember that it is a vision I am relating.) It was this: Would it be possible for me to obtain permission to go back to the world, to that very part of it from which I had come, clothed in some human form, and live my earthly life over again — live it in a manner worthy of my profession, worthy of my Christ and my opportunity? Could this be?

If at that moment an answer in the affirmative had been brought to me, I would have gladly given up my heavenly blessedness. I would have gladly undergone ages of hardship, ignominy, poverty and pain. I would have given up a million dollars in money. Yes, I would have gladly given a world, if it had been mine to give! But I could see no hope for a second probation. What was to be done?

I had not been musing in this way for many seconds, for thoughts appeared to flow with remarkable rapidity, when, quick as a lightning flash, one of those bright inhabitants which I had watched floating far off in the clouds of glory, descended and stood before my astonished gaze.

I can never forget the awe-struck feelings with which I beheld this heavenly being. Describe the shape and features and bearing of this noble form I cannot, and will not attempt it. He was at the same time angelic and human, earthly and yet celestial. I discerned therefore at a glance that he was one of the "blood-washed multitude" who had "come out of the great tribulations of earth." I not only judged from a certain majestic appearance which he bore, but from instinct I felt that the being before me was a man, a redeemed and glorified man.

He looked at me. And I could not keep from returning his gaze. His eyes compelled me. And I confess I was ravished by his beauty. I could never have believed the human face divine could ever bear so grand a stamp of dignity and charm.

But far beyond the entrancing loveliness of those celestial features was the expression which filled his total countenance, and shone through those eyes that were gazing upon me. It was as though that face was only a sunlit window, through which I could see into the depths of the pure, kindly and tender soul within.

I don't know how I looked to my beautiful visitor. I don't know what form I had. I had not seen myself in a mirror since I had taken on immortality for mortality.

It was evident that he had a deep interest in me. But it was an interest which seemed to bring sadness to him. His features seemed to me to grow almost sorrowful as I sat there with my eyes fixed on him in a fascinated spell.

He spoke first. Had he not done so I could never have summoned courage to address him. His voice was soft and musical, and fitted well with the seriousness of his bearing. I understood him almost before I heard his words, although I cannot tell now what language he spoke. I suppose it was the universal language of heaven.

This was the substance of what he said: My arrival was known throughout a certain district of the celestial regions, where were gathered the ransomed ones who had come from the earthly neighborhood where I had lived. The tidings of my arrival had been flashed through the heavenly telephone, which spoke not in one ear only, but in every ear in that particular region. My name had been whispered in every hillside and echoed in every valley, and had been spoken in every room of every mansion. It had been proclaimed from every tower and pinnacle of the stupendous temple in which these glorified saints day and night present their worship to the great Father.

All who had known me on earth, all who had any knowledge of my family, my opportunities for helping forward the Kingdom of Christ, whom they worshipped and adored, were burning to see me and hear me tell of the victories I had won and the souls I had blessed while on earth. And all were especially anxious to hear if I had been the means of bringing salvation to the loved ones they had left behind.

All this was poured upon my soul. I didn't know which way to look. Again and again I remembered my life of ease and comfort. What could I say? How could I appear with the record of my life before these waiting ones? What was there in it except a record of self-gratification? I had no martyr stories to tell. I had sacrificed nothing worth naming on earth, much less in heaven, for His dear sake!

My mind was running in this direction when I think my visitor must have discovered something of what I was thinking, and felt pity for me. Seeing my consternation, he spoke again.

"Where you find yourself is not actually heaven," he said, "but only its forecourt, a sort of outer circle. Presently, the Lord Himself, with a great procession of His chosen ones will come to take you into the Celestial City itself. There is where your residence will be if He deems you worthy; that is, if your conduct on the battlefield below has pleased Him.

"Meanwhile, I have obtained permission to come and speak to you concerning a soul who is very dear to me. I understand he lives in the neighborhood where you recently lived, and from which have just come. Our knowledge of the affairs of earth is, for our own sakes, limited, but now and then we are permitted to get a glimpse.

"Can you," he said, "tell me anything about my son? He was my only son. I loved him dearly. I loved him too much.

I spoiled him when a child! He had his own way. He grew up willful, passionate and disobedient. And my example didn't help him."

Here a cloud for a moment came over the beautiful brow, but vanished as quickly as it came. "Memory has been busy, but that has all gone," he said, as though talking to himself. And then he finished the story of his prodigal son. He, the father, had been rescued, washed, regenerated. He had learned to fight for souls, and had won many to the blood-stained banner. Then he had suddenly been taken in death by an accident at his work and was taken to Heaven.

"And now," he added, "where is my boy? Give me tidings of my boy! He lived near you, and had business dealings with you. What did you do for him? Is there hope? Tell me what his feelings are today."

He stopped speaking. My heart sank within me. What could I say? I knew the boy. The story of the father's death and his prodigal son had been told me. I had never spoken one serious word to the boy about his soul or about his Savior. I had been busy about other things. And now, what could I say to his father, who stood before me? I was speechless!

The cloud that I had noticed before again came over the face of my visitor, but with a dark shadow this time. He must have guessed the truth. He looked at me with a look in which I felt that disappointment to himself and pity for me were combined. He then spread his wings and soared away.

I was so intently gazing after his retreating form that I hadn't noticed a second fair being, who had descended from above, and who now occupied the place abandoned only a moment before by my last visitor.

I turned and looked upon the newcomer. This was a spirit of the same class, of the same ransomed multitude who once were dwellers on earth. There was a dignity of bearing, the same marvelous expression of inward power, purity, and joy. But in this case there was a beauty (which I could have imagined) of more delicate and enthralling mold.

Beautiful as I thought my first visitor to be, more beautiful than conception or dream of earth could be, yet here was a beauty that surpassed it — not, perhaps, if judged from heaven's view, but judged from my standpoint, for it must be remembered that I was still a man. My former visitor I have said was a glorious man — this one was evidently the glorified form of a woman.

I had, when on earth, sometimes thought that I could have wished for the privilege of beholding Eve in the hour when she came forth from the hands of her Maker. And I had imagined something — only something, of what her beautiful form must have been as she sprang into being on that bridal morning, young and pure and beautiful — the fair image of her Maker — perhaps, the sweetest work of God. Now, here I saw her — I saw Eve reproduced before my eyes as young, pure and beautiful, even more beautiful than her first mother could possibly have been, for was not this His finished work?

But I was soon awakened from my dream by the voice of the fair creature who, from her manner, evidently wished to speak to me on some matter of great importance.

She told me her name. I had heard it on earth. She was a widow who had struggled through great difficulties. Her husband's death had resulted in her conversion to Christ. Converted, she had given herself up unreservedly to fight for the Lord. Her children had been her first care. They had all been saved, and were fighting for God, except one.

The mention of that name brought the same saddening cloud on her lovely face which had dimmed the bright face of my first visitor. But the cloud vanished almost as soon as it came. That one, that unsaved one, was a girl who had been her mother's delight. She had grown up beautiful, the village pride, but alas! had gone astray. It was the old story of wrong, and of being seduced into evil ways. And then of utter abandonment to that way of life, and all the consequent train of miseries.

I listened. I had known some of the sad story on earth, but I had turned away from hearing any more about it as

91

being "no concern of mine." Little did I ever think that I would be confronted with it in heaven!

And now the bright spirit turned those eyes on me that, beaming with love and concern, were more beautiful than ever. She said again: "My daughter lived near you. You know her. Have you saved her? I don't know much about her, but I do know that one earnest and determined effort would save her, and win her to Christ."

And then again she asked me, "Have you saved my child?"

I must have cried out in agony. I know I put my hands over my eyes, because I could no longer bear to meet her intent look, which now turned to one of pity for me.

How long she continued to look on me, with an expression of concern almost greater than she had shown for her lost child, I do not know. But when I uncovered my eyes, she was gone, and the silvery sheen of her white wings marked her out to my seeking eyes like a speck on the distant blue.

Then I cried out, "Oh, my God, is this heaven? Will these questionings go on forever? Will the meanness and selfishness of my past life haunt me throughout eternity? What shall I do? Can I not go back to earth, and do something to redeem myself from this wretched sense of unworthiness? Can I not live my life over again?"

This question had hardly passed through my mind when there was another rush of wings, and down beside me alighted another form, surprisingly resembling the first that had spoken to me, and yet, oh so very different! But I will not take time to describe him; you must imagine it.

He introduced himself much in the same way as my former visitors. He had been a great singer, but was awakened and won to Christ only a short while back. Having had much forgiven, he had loved much. All his desire after his conversion was to get free from the entanglements of business and to devote himself a living sacrifice to the saving of men.

When just on the threshold of the realization of his wish, he had been sent to heaven. And here he was, a spirit of glory and joy, coming to inquire of me concerning the church group among whom he had labored, and of the crowd of companions he had left behind. Was I acquainted with his little church? Their place of worship was near my place of business. Had I helped them in their difficulties, and in their service and testimony for Christ? Had I done anything for his old mates, who were drinking and cursing their way to hell? He had died with prayers for them on his lips. Had I stopped them on their way to ruin?

Again I could not speak. What could I say? I knew his church. But I had never given them any encouragement or help. I knew of the hovels in which his old mates lived, and the dens of hell in which they spent their time and money. But I had been too busy, or too proud, or too cowardly to seek them out with the message of the Savior's love.

I was utterly speechless. He guessed my feelings, I suppose, because with a look of sympathy he left in sadness — at least in as much sadness as is possible in heaven.

As for myself, I was in anguish — strange as it may appear, considering I was in heaven. But so it was. Wondering whether there was not some comfort for me, I involuntarily looked around. And I saw a marvelous phenomenon on the horizon at a great distance. All that part of the heavens appeared to be filled with a brilliant light, surpassing the blaze of a thousand suns at noonday. And yet there was no blinding glare making it difficult to gaze upon, as is the case with our own sun when it shines in its glory. Here was a brilliance far surpassing anything that could be imagined, and yet I could look upon it with pleasure.

As I continued to gaze, wondering what it could be, it appeared to come a little closer. Then I realized it was coming in my direction. I was still reclining on the banks of the beautiful river.

And now I could distinctly hear the sound of music. The distance was a great many miles, after the measurement of earth, but the atmosphere was so clear, and I found my eyesight so strong, that I could easily see objects at a distance which, on earth, would have required a powerful telescope.

The sound came closer. It was music, beyond question — and such music as I had never heard before. But there was a strange commingling of other sounds which all together made a marvelous melody, made up, as I afterwards discovered, by the strains that came from the multitude of musicians, and the shouts and songs that proceeded from innumerable voices. This phenomenon was approaching rapidly. But my curiosity was so strongly aroused to know what it was, that a few minutes seemed an age.

Finally I was able to make out what it was. It was astounding! But who could describe it! The whole firmament was filled, as it were, with innumerable forms, each of beauty and dignity, far surpassing those with whom I had already made an acquaintance. Here was a representative portion of the aristocracy of heaven accompanying the King, who came to welcome into the heaven of heavens the spirits of men and women who had escaped from earth, who had fought the good fight, who had kept the faith, and had overcome in the conflict as He had overcome.

I stood filled with awe and wonder. Could it be possible? Was I at last actually to see my Lord and be welcomed by Him? In the thought of this rapture I forgot the sorrow that only a moment before had reigned in my heart, and my whole nature swelled with expectation and delight.

And now the procession was upon me. I had seen some of the pageants of earth — displays that required the power of mighty monarchs, and the wealth of great cities and nations to create — but they were each, or all combined, as the feeble light of a candle to a tropical sun in comparison with the tremendous scene which now spread itself before my astonished eyes.

On it came. I had sprung up from my reclining position, and then had fallen prostrate as the first rank of these shining heavenly spirits neared me. Each one looked in himself, to my untutored eyes, like a god, so far as greatness and power could be expressed by the outward appearance of any being.

Rank after rank swept past me. Each turned his eyes upon me, or seemed to do so. I could not help feeling that I was somewhat an object of pity to them all. Perhaps it was my own feelings that made me imagine this. But it certainly appeared to me as though these noble beings regarded me as a fearful, cowardly soul, who had only cared for his own interests on earth, and had come up there with the same selfish motives.

On they came. Thousands passed me, yet there appeared to me to be no diminishment in the numbers yet to come. I looked at the procession as it stretched backwards, but my eyes could see no end to it. There must have been millions. It was indeed a "multitude that no man could number."

All were praising God, either in hymns expressive of adoration and worship, or by recounting, in songs of rapture the mighty victories which they had witnessed on earth — or describing some wonderful work they had seen elsewhere.

And now, the great central glory and attraction of the splendid procession was at hand.

I gathered this from the still more dignified character of the beings who now swept by, the heavier crash of music and the louder shouts of exultation which came pealing from all around.

I was right, and before I could prepare my spirit for the visitation, it was upon me. The King was here! In the center of circling hosts — which rose tier above tier into the blue vault above, turning on Him their millions of eyes, lustrous with the love they bore Him — I beheld the celestial form of Him who once died for me upon the cross. The procession halted. Then at a word of command, they formed up instantly in three sides of a square in front of me, the King standing in the center immediately opposite the spot where I had prostrated myself.

What a sight that was! Worth toiling a lifetime to behold it! Nearest to the King were the patriarchs and apostles of ancient times. Next, rank after rank, came the holy martyrs who had died for Him. Then came the army of warriors who had fought for Him in every part of the world.

And around and about, above and below, I beheld myriads and myriads of spirits who were never heard of on earth outside their own neighborhood, or beyond their own times, who, with self-denying zeal and untiring toil had labored to extend God's Kingdom and to save the souls of men. And encircling the gorgeous scene, above, beneath, around, hovered glittering angelic beings who had kept their first estate, proud, it seemed to me, to minister to the happiness and exaltation of these redeemed out of the poor world from which I came.

I was bewildered by the scene. The songs, the music, the shouts of the multitude that came like the roar of a thousand cataracts, echoed and re-echoed through the sunlit mountains. And the magnificent and endless array of happy spirits ravished my senses with passionate delight. All at once, however, I remembered myself, and was reminded of the High Presence before Whom I was bowed, and lifting up my eyes I beheld Him gazing upon me.

What a look it was! It was not pain, and yet it was not pleasure. It was not anger, and yet it was not approval. Anyway, I felt that in that face, so inexpressibly admirable and glorious, there was yet no welcome for me. I had felt this in the faces of my previous visitors. I felt it again in the Lord's.

That face, that Divine face, seemed to say to me, for language was not needed to convey to the very depths of my soul what His feelings were to me: "Thou wilt feel thyself little in harmony with these, once the companions of My tribulations and now of My glory, who counted not their lives dear unto themselves in order that they might bring honor to Me and salvation to men." And He gave a look of admiration at the host of apostles and martyrs and warriors gathered around Him.

Oh, that look of Jesus! I felt that to have one such loving recognition — it would be worth dying a hundred deaths at the stake. It would be worth being torn asunder by wild beasts. The angelic escort felt it too, for their responsive burst of praise and song shook the very skies and the ground on which I lay.

Then the King turned His eyes on me again. How I wished that some mountain would fall upon me and hide me forever from His presence! But I wished in vain. Some invisible and irresistible force compelled me to look up, and my eyes met His once more. I felt, rather than heard, Him saying to me in words that engraved themselves as fire upon my brain:

"Go back to earth. I will give thee another opportunity. Prove thyself worthy of My name. Show to the world that thou possessest My spirit by doing My works, and becoming, on My behalf, a savior of men. Thou shalt return hither when thou hast finished the battle, and I will give thee a place in My conquering train, and a share in My glory."

What I felt under that look and those words, no heart or mind could possibly describe. They were mingled feelings. First came the unutterable anguish arising out of the full realization that I had wasted my life, that it had been a life squandered on the paltry ambitions and trifling pleasures of earth — while it might have been filled and sown with deeds that would have produced a never-ending harvest of heavenly fruit. My life could have won for me the approval of heaven's King, and made me worthy to be the companion of these glorified heroes.

But combined with this self-reproach there was a gleam of hope. My earnest desire to return to earth was to be granted. Perhaps it was in response to the longings I had felt ever since the realization of my earthly failures had dawned upon me that this favor was granted to me. I could have the privilege of living my life over again. True, it was a high responsibility, but Jesus would be with me. His Spirit would enable me. And in my heart I felt ready to face it.

The cloud of shining ones had vanished. The music was silent. I closed my eyes and gave myself over, body, soul and spirit, to the disposal of my Savior — to live, not for my own salvation, but for the glory of my Christ, and for the salvation of the world. And then and there, the same blessed voice of my King stole over my heart, as He promised that His presence should go with me back to earth, and make me more than [a] conqueror through His blood.